A Sindhi Mother's Cookbook

With best Compliments
Durru Sachdev

A Sindhi Mother's Cookbook

A woman's love for her family expressed through food

Duru Sachdev

PRABHAT
PRAKASHAN

Published by
PRABHAT PRAKASHAN PVT. LTD.
4/19 Asaf Ali Road,
New Delhi-110 002 (INDIA)
e-mail: prabhatbooks@gmail.com

ISBN 978-93-95386-26-5
A SINDHI MOTHER'S COOKBOOK
by Smt. Duru Sachdev

Edition
2025

Price
₹ 600.00 (Rupees Six Hundred only)

Printed at
R-Tech Offset Printers, Delhi

Mother, Daughter and Grand-daughter

My Grandchildren

पूजितं ह्यशनं नित्यं बलं ऊर्जं च यच्छति।
अपूजितं तु तद्भुक्तं उभयं नाशयेदिदम्।।

—मनुस्मृतिः

आदरपूर्वक किया हुआ भोजन सदैव बल और स्फूर्ति देने वाला होता है और अनादरपूर्वक खाया हुआ बल और स्फूर्ति दोनों को नष्ट करता है।

—मनुस्मृतिः

'Food, thus worshipped, always imparts strength and vigour; if eaten irreverently, it destroys both.'

—Manusmriti

SINDH: FROM WHERE IT ALL STARTED

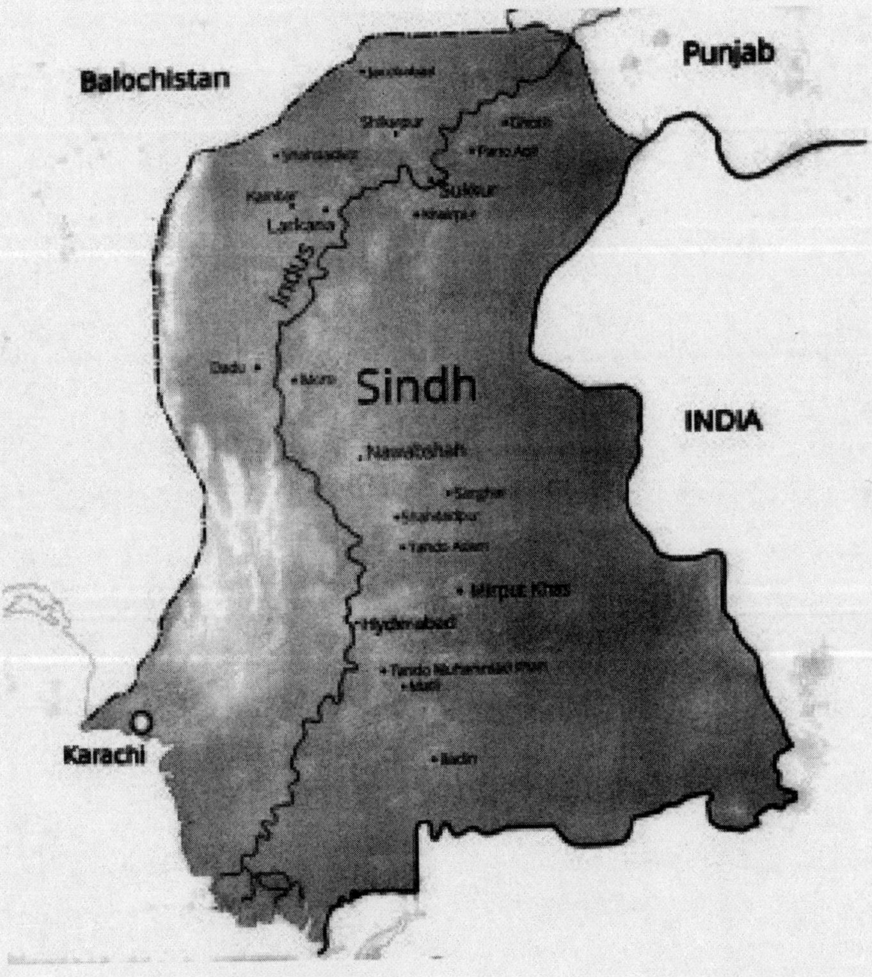

FOREWORD

How does one express appreciation to a partner and companion—someone who has stood by your side through life's ups and downs, through all the pains and pleasures? I do not know if words are adequate; what I do know is that I have been given the opportunity to acknowledge one aspect of my wife's steadfast presence in my life and I must try and find the words.

It is a fact that most of us take these efficient time-managers, skilled artists, master chefs, the joy-givers who are true 'homemakers', for granted and often forget to appreciate or express our gratitude. I am no different. For 50 years, as I filled my life with work and business, Duru created a home—one I took for granted, never questioning or seeing the labour of love that goes into being 'just a homemaker'. It is not that she did not venture out into the world—she did and succeeded admirably in her business ventures as well but, like so many of my generation, I did not see my wife as an individual, as a strong, independent woman, despite the fact that she most certainly is one. When I look back, I do not recall a single moment when I shared a compliment or a word of appreciation. I was her biggest critic, quick to find fault and point it out—so that she could 'improve'.

As I have grown older and, I like to think, wiser, I wonder at my arrogance in failing to acknowledge and appreciate the contribution of my partner in life; for taking it all for granted; for believing that, after all she was only doing her 'duty'. It has been brought home to me now, when I see that, while I am enjoying the slower pace of my retirement, Duru still has the energy and passion to venture into new territories. This is a foreword to her recipe book, so let me distil my appreciation from just that one facet of her multifaceted personality.

It has been an unwritten rule in our house that every dish must always be homemade and let us not underestimate just how relentless and laborious the task of planning and preparing daily meals is, even for one who enjoys cooking. Despite that, I always found Duru efficiently and cheerfully serving up the most sumptuous and wholesome meals for all of us. Be it for a small family dinner or a large get-together, with extended family and friends joining us for a planned or a surprise party, the table would be immaculately laid and a beaming smile on the face of the lady of the house. Even today, despite so many thankless years, she still loves to experiment, cook something special and provide a joyful culinary experience to whoever graces her table. No wonder our home is a popular choice for get-togethers!

I can see now that it has been the kitchen and the dining table that has nurtured our family. There was food not only for our stomachs but for our minds—not just for our bodies but for our souls. Eating meals together created a sense of security and harmony. It was where experiences, ideas and feelings were shared, problems were solved and values imparted. It was mealtimes that created the bonds that enhanced relationships.

Today I look around and see small, nuclear families where each member is so preoccupied, or should I say driven, by their own lives that they seldom 'see' each other; where families interact on social media, wish each other through chat or messages; where living apart and far away seems a 'less stressful' option for many.

I am forced to ask myself, by taking for granted the efforts of the woman of the house, by negating all her efforts, did I, along with so many others like me, erase her as a possible role model for the next generation? I hope not. I truly believe that she deserves the highest respect. The world will be a sadder place without those such as her.

I am blessed to have Duru as my life partner and I am proud of her and her achievements. I hope the irresistible flavour of her recipes will be relished by all of you and your families as it has been by us all these years.

—Sudesh Sachdev

FOR MY FAMILY

The spirit to challenge oneself and accomplish something that we never thought possible is supremely empowering and today I feel empowered.

I am a homemaker. My forte is cooking. I consider cooking an art. I picked up the nuances of this art from my mother and mother-in-law. As I observed them cook, I would be fascinated by how a slight change in ingredients, the stage of the process at which they were added, could totally change the flavour of the end product. I was touched by the love and patience with which they would cook for the family and how their faces would light up each time we commented on how good something was! Unknowingly, I developed a love for cooking and, once I took charge of my own home, felt most comfortable in the kitchen. That I would one day pen down the recipes handed down to me, was unimaginable. Yet, here I am, doing just that! And it's turning out to be a lot of fun.

So why did I set out on this unfamiliar journey of writing a cookbook of Sindhi recipes?

I could say it all started when I married into a large, close-knit family. We would often entertain large gatherings and food was always the high point. My mother-in-law, other ladies of the family and I, would cook Sindhi recipes handed down through generations, recalling not just traditional lifestyle and hospitality, but also memories of the 'old life' in what is now Pakistan—recipes and memories that have stayed with me that I would like to share with my children and my children's children.

I could say it all started when my daughter was in USA for higher studies. She asked me to write down recipes so that she could try to cook there. I wrote down many and gave them to her. One day, while going through all my files, full of recipes and notes that I had written for my daughter, I decided to update the notes, add more recipes and rewrite many of them.

I could say that my children, including my son-in law and daughter-in-law, have been pestering me to write. Whenever they come home for lunch or dinner and I cook a meal of their choice, the topic of me putting together a book of recipes just has to come up.

All those reasons would be true and yet, by themselves they would not have persuaded me to go so far out of my comfort zone. I am willing to try anything in the kitchen—that is my domain. However, real time cooking and writing about it are two different things altogether. I am a home-cook. I do not use measuring spoons and cups while cooking. Rather, I go by instinct—good old-fashioned *andaza.*

Present

For me, cooking is not solely about ingredients and method and serving tips; it is about serving and feeding one's family and loved ones, nurturing the mind, body and soul. It is about the food but more about the memories: the aromas that led children and adults straight from the front door to the kitchen with the question, 'What's cooking?' The recollections of a laughing child tossing a hot 'pakora' from hand to hand; of two tiffins tucked into a schoolbag—one to be 'stolen' by peers in the school bus, the other to ensure my children did not go hungry; of a preteen sitting on the kitchen slab, sharing his/her day; of a house full of noisy, playful children demanding to be fed, secure in the knowledge that they would always get their favourite dish; of my granddaughter's entitled request: '*Nani*, curd rice, please'; of a toddler marching in, stating confidently: '*Dadi, bhook!*' (Grandma, I'm hungry!)

For me, my kitchen is the heart of the family. It binds everyone together with love shared in the form of food. I observe the influence of interactions and conversations at the dining table. The mingling of ages, interests and experiences as dishes pass from hand to hand; sharing, minding of manners, being appreciative—there is so much to be learnt while filling the stomach. How can a recipe book bind within its covers all these memories, emotions, feelings?

I look around today and it saddens me when, among other things, I see people forgetting to appreciate what they put into their bodies in their restless search for convenience and efficiency. Food is now a commodity, to be ordered remotely, served on disposable dishes and eaten with throwaway cutlery. Fast food, the ingredients and preparation of which do not bear investigation, is the new norm. It fills the stomach but in what form will it reach the heart and soul, if at all? We are what we eat. Neglecting how or what we eat is the same as neglecting our bodies and by neglecting our bodies, we are neglecting our minds.

Past

So, this is a book of Sindhi recipes—dishes that my family and friends have enjoyed over the years. I was born after the Partition of the subcontinent, in India, but my parents and in-laws, all came from Sindh, located in the south-eastern region of what is now Pakistan.

The region is defined by River Indus (the word *sind* is derived from the Sanskrit *sindhu* meaning 'river') and the rich alluvial soil with which it fertilises the plains it flows through. On the eastern fringe lies the Thar desert and to the west rise the Kirthar mountains. It was here that the Indus Valley civilisation and the towns of Mohenjo Daro and Harappa flourished. Kings and kingdoms of Sind are referred to in the epic *Mahabharata.* In 325 BC, it was here on the banks of the Indus that the Greek army commanded by Alexander the Great set up camp. It was the Greeks who referred to the land east of the Indus as *Hind.*

The rich plains of the Indus attracted many. Sindh was ruled by Mauryans, (Ashoka introduced Buddhism to the region), the Kushans, the Guptas as well as more regional dynasties, such as the Chachars of Alor. Muhammad bin Qasim conquered the valley of Indus in AD 712, bringing with him Islam and the rule of the Arab Caliphate.

But this is not meant to be a lesson in Sindhi history. I am looking back to my heritage to trace the strong influences on Sindhi food. Over the years, a cuisine that must have been based on the abundance of fresh produce the Indus and alluvial plains around it ensured—vegetables as well as meat and fresh-water fish—integrated flavours from as far away as Greece, Central Asia, as well as the eastern Gangetic Plains.

The Partition of the subcontinent was heart-breaking, as much for the Sindhis as for any of the other displaced community. We left our homeland in Pakistan and can now only carry it with us in our hearts and minds. That is another reason I want to keep the flavours of Sindh alive for our children.

Over a million Sindhis left their homeland for India, eventually settling across the length and breadth of the country, and around the globe. Today, Sindhi communities can be found in Kolkata, Ludhiana, Mumbai, Coimbatore Dubai, Toronto, Sydney, Singapore... as first- and second-generation migrants, we were aware of our culture and identity but today, particularly in more cosmopolitan areas, differences have blurred. Today, traditions, including the cuisine, are slowly and subtly overlaid and imbued with local, even global, flavours—chicken did not feature on the traditional menu, though today it has established a niche for itself; the fresh spring garlic that gave dishes such a delicate, piquant twist is almost forgotten and its place taken by more robust garlic cloves.

And not just that ... so much more is being forgotten, or lost to popular culture—how many know that Hyderabadi 'biryani' also gets its name from Hyderabad in Sindh, my mother's hometown, the heart of a rich, rice-growing region on the banks of the Indus, where the fragrant, long-grained Basmati flourishes?

And Future

This cookbook is my humble tribute to Sindhi cuisine and my love for it. It is written to share and hand down to the next generation what I learnt from my parents and in-laws, who learnt from theirs. To remind them that 'lolos' are intrinsic to the celebration of Thadri, just as on Cheti Chand, Lord Jhulelal's birthday, boiled 'channa' and 'tayhri' is what was traditionally served.

I have consciously adhered to the 'Sindhi' cooking style, and, as I translate intuitive measures into cups, tablespoons and teaspoons, I hope to evoke the aromas and flavours of a heritage that are gradually dissipating. All the recipes included are in the Sindhi tradition, with an emphasis on the flavour of the main ingredient—'masalas', freshly ground and fragrant, are all supporting acts that should never overwhelm the main ingredient. I have included simple, basic sweets, much loved by my children when they were young and now appreciated by their children, despite the wide variety of sweets and desserts now available.

Make no mistake, I am not a purist. I know that times have changed and that it is not always realistic to prepare lengthy meals every day. I use a pressure cooker and refrigerate pre-cooked 'masalas'—just in case—as well, and I have included these in my recipes. As I said earlier, it is not just the food—it is the kitchen, the cooking and, most of all, the cook that defines the flavours that are served and linger in our memories.

So, here I am, accepting the challenging task of not only handing down recipes of traditional Sindhi food but also the warmth and love with which the traditional kitchen nurtured the family.

Hubh sa sabhni vaste!
(From my heart to all of you!)

—Duru Sachdev

BEFORE YOU BEGIN

I would like to highlight some key factors to keep in mind when you are cooking. While some of these tips are more relevant to the recipes featured in this book, others hold true for most cooking styles. What is important is the understanding that a meal, however simple, is not something to be just 'put together' mindlessly, in a hurry. Food nourishes the soul even in preparation. Take the time, think about a balance of colours and of flavours, and you will find the end result so much more enjoyable.

Buy Fresh

I still follow the old tradition of buying fresh vegetables on a day-to-day basis as far as possible and preparing meals using fresh vegetables and locally grown food.

I urge you to try cooking with freshly bought vegetables and make the same recipes with vegetables stored in the refrigerator for one week. With my experience, I can share that there is definitely a difference in taste as well as the nutritional value of the food. Storing food in the refrigerator for days is not conducive to healthy eating and, therefore, should be avoided. It changes the taste of both cooked and raw food as the vegetables and fruits lose some quantity of water, taste and nutritional value.

Buying Vegetables

It is quite a task to select the best of the 'fresh' produce from a vegetable cart or vendor. I always pick up and feel the vegetables, checking to make sure that they do not have any cuts or dirty spots on the surface—a tiny, discoloured hole could indicate a worm in residence! There should be brightness to the skin and flesh should be firm and not over-ripe or mushy.

For example, if you are buying 'Simla mirch', gently feel the edge of the cap on top. It should be firm and not soft and squishy. 'Bheeh' (lotus stem) should be thick and round and if you scrape off a bit of the skin, the flesh under it should be almost white in colour. When buying 'meha' (Indian squash), buy the ones that have a slightly fuzzy skin as these are the tender, juicier ones. Weigh a round 'vangan' (brinjal) in your hand and buy the lighter one as it will not have seeds and taste better. Check 'bheendyun' (okra) by bending the 'tail'—if it snaps off easily, the 'bheendyun' is soft and fresh, not stringy.

However, be considerate while satisfying yourself of the quality—the vendor will not appreciate your damaging his produce in the process.

Cleaning and Cutting

Always wash vegetables and fruit thoroughly with clean water, even if they are individually wrapped and appear to be very clean. If you are removing the skin, wash the vegetable once again. For leafy greens, such as saag, remove and clean the stringy stems from the leaves and edible portions, then wash two to three times before chopping. Do not wash after chopping as nutrients may be lost. Remember, some vegetables, such as 'bheendyun' can become gooey or very sticky if cut when wet or washed after being cut. Make sure they are dry before cutting them.

Buying Masalas

It is as important to buy 'masalas' with utmost care. The quality of 'masalas' affects the taste of the dish you are preparing. My experience has taught me to buy pure 'masalas' from a reliable, branded store or company. Most spices are quite expensive, but it is worth spending that much more to buy quality, as you will use a smaller amount of the spice but get better flavours. Adulteration in powdered spices is quite common, which is why, in some cases it is better to buy whole spice, sun dry or roast it slightly and then grind it at home. Traditionally, 'masalas' would be freshly ground every day as needed, but that is not possible today—just make sure, you store them in airtight containers.

Cooking on a Low Flame

There are a few principles of cooking which I have followed strictly. The first and foremost is to cook on a low flame. My father-in-law, who loved food and enjoyed preparing it as well, was very particular about cooking on a low flame. The reason was scientific. Cooking on a low flame enables the vegetables, pulses, etc, to be cooked completely from the inside without burning the crust. It requires fewer spices, thus retaining the natural flavour of the main ingredient. There is another reason for low-flame cooking and that is that the food cooked like this not only retains more nutrients, but is light on the stomach, easy to digest and, therefore, allows the body to absorb more nutrition. One tiny bite was enough for my father-in-law to tell that this rule had been broken while preparing a dish. Over time, I picked up his 'cooking philosophy' and made it my own.

'Bhuno' (Fry)

The word 'bhuno', or 'bhunna', refers to a particular process of removing excess water and browning 'masalas' or vegetables in 'ghee' or oil. Thus, a 'basar-tamata' (onion-tomato) 'masala' could be 'bhuno-ed', as could a preparation of 'saag-patata' (leafy greens-potato). The process involves heating the requisite amount of 'ghee' or oil in a '*kadhai*', adding the 'masala' or vegetable and then cooking over a low flame. Stirring is critical to ensure even browning and to prevent the 'masala' or vegetable from sticking to the sides and burning. The 'masala' or vegetable is 'bhuno-ed' till it changes colour and starts giving out oil on the edges.

'Tadka'

Another basic process in South Asian cooking, 'tadka' translates as 'tempering'—adding whole spices to hot oil or 'ghee' in order to extract the maximum flavour and aroma and infuse it in the dish. 'Tadka' can start the cooking process or end it. In my recipes, I have used the term to refer to the final step in the cooking process of some dishes. For that, a small, heavy pan or a special long-handled ladle is used. 'Ghee' or oil is heated in it till smoky hot, then the spices are added and the whole submerged in the dish which is covered instantly to retain the smoky aromas. Speed is of the essence in this process as the spices must not burn in the hot oil but be brown-ed.

Using 'Haldi'

The addition of 'haldi' (turmeric) to the daily diet has many scientifically proven benefits. It aids digestion, fights inflammation, gives relief from pain, improves memory and heals the body from within. The spice has been an integral part of the cuisine of this region for centuries. However, it is important to know how to use it correctly. I suggest that you never add 'haldi' to hot 'ghee' or oil directly as it will burn and impart a bitter aftertaste to the dish. 'Haldi' should be added with other 'masalas', slightly later in the cooking process so that it gently releases its goodness. Also, keep in mind that 'haldi' has a very strong natural colour and this will influence the final look of the dish. Use sparingly, especially, in dark, leafy vegetables and green 'dal' to avoid dull, dark overtones.

'Garam Masala'

'Garam'—literally hot—refers to the intrinsic quality of the spices that comprise this mix of spices. They are 'hot', not necessarily on the tongue but in the way they affect the body. While various brands sell readymade 'garam masala', I prefer to make my own and have included my tried and tested mix of spices in the recipes. Since the flavour and aroma of each spice included is so distinctive, I recommend that you should try to grind it fresh. If you prefer to store it, make sure that the container you are using is airtight and don't store the 'masala' for too long. 'Garam masala' is best added last, just a little, sprinkled as a garnish before the dish is served. If added earlier in the cooking process, it may change the colour of the dish.

When Things Go Wrong

Oil, chilli and salt are cooking ingredients that enhance the flavour of any dish—unfortunately, if not used with a controlled, balanced hand, they can also ruin it. So, if when checking out the results of your efforts in the kitchen, you discover that you have been a little heavy-handed and the dish is fit to be consumed only by the trash can, here are some tips on how you could save it.

Too Much Chilli or Salt

If the dish is a dry one, you can add a few drops of lemon juice or dry mango powder. The sourness added will balance excess chilli or salt.

For a gravy, cut a potato into four and add it to the gravy and let it simmer. The potato will absorb some of the gravy together with the excess chilli and salt. If required, add a little more water and simmer some more. Remove the potato before serving.

Another trick is to add a tablespoon of flour, or balls of dough, to the gravy and boil it. The flour will absorb the salt, and eventually float to the top. Remove carefully with a strainer before serving the dish.

If the gravy is a little thick, you could try adding a little boiling water and then simmering the whole for two minutes. This will dilute the excess somewhat.

A tablespoon or two of coconut milk or cream can be a saviour as well. Both give the dish a richer texture and taste, while cooling chilli and salt.

A few spoons of whipped curd will also do the same—but curd may affect the flavour of the dish.

Not Enough Salt

It is easy enough to add additional salt to a gravy once it is cooked, but what if it is 'biryani' or a dry dish? Take the lid of the cooking vessel, which will have drops of water condensed on the inside and spread salt on it. Cover the vessel once again and simmer for two to three minutes. The steam that forms in the vessel will cause the salt to disperse evenly.

Too Much Oil

The easiest way to remove excess oil is to tilt the vessel and scoop it out. However, this may a bit messy.

If you have the time, what works well is to refrigerate the dish. The extra oil will cool and coagulate on top. It can then be easily removed with a spoon.

A tablespoon of flour in the gravy will also absorb extra oil as it boils. Lumps of flour will gradually float up to the surface from where they can be removed with a strainer.

Another option is to drop in a clean, fibre tissue which will absorb the oil very quickly. Do remember to remove it before serving!

Myths and Beliefs

Fish

Sindh is home to the much-celebrated *palla* fish (*Tenualosa ilisha,* also known as hilsa) and 'fish pulao' is enjoyed in many households. But there are also many myths about eating fish that abound. The most common of these is that drinking milk or eating a milk product after a meal that features fish will result in white patches on the skin. Leucoderma is a skin disorder that causes skin to lose its pigmentation and form whites patches in several area. There is absolutely no scientific evidence to prove the link between eating fish and leucoderma.

Another myth holds that fish should be eaten only in months that have an 'r' in their name, which means that in May, June, July and August, fish-based dishes should not be consumed. This may have some scientific basis because May to August is the breeding season during which fish produce a certain toxin and it is better not to consume it as this toxin is harmful to the health.

'Taseer'

Another popular belief speaks of the innate properties—'taseer'—of different foods as hot or cold. Too much hot 'taseer' food is considered unhealthy as it is believed that it aggravates the hot-blooded side of one's nature. Eating foods with a cold 'taseer' in winter will naturally make one more susceptible to cold. Curd is cold, as is rice—Sindhis eat rice for lunch in winter and for dinner in summer. Fish is said to have a hot 'taseer', which could be another reason why eating it during the hot summer months is discouraged.

Traditional Combinations

Then of course, there are some foods that must be eaten together to get the most in terms of both nutrition and taste. Close to the hearts of Sindhi's everywhere are combinations, such as

kadhi with took and rice
sai bhaji with papad and khichadi
pakwan with channa dal and dahi
moong dal with poori
mithi seviyaan and fried aloo
koki with dahi, achar and/or papad
dal-chhola with dhabal
kutti with papad.

Utensils

'Kadhai'

No Indian kitchen would be complete without a *'kadhai'*; in fact, most have more than one—in different sizes, weights, as well as materials. The circular, concave vessel has a deep curved bottom that rises smoothy up to a wide mouth—very similar in shape to the Chinese wok. It is used for both sauteing and deep frying. The curved base that sits on the flame is where heat is concentrated; the open, curved sides of the *'kadhai'* allow heat to dissipate, while the circular smoothness of the vessel makes for quick, easy stirring of ingredients in and out of the hot area, supporting the 'bhuno-ing' or frying that is characteristic of Indian cooking.

Heavy-bottom Pan

An absolute essential for slow cooking, the heavy base of the pan heats up slowly and retains heat for long, allowing sustained and even cooking on a low flame.

Pressure Cooker

Irreplaceable in the Indian kitchen today, the pressure cooker rules simply by virtue of having reduced the cooking time of foods by half, while retaining their nutritional value. Steam trapped inside the cooker raises the internal pressure and with it the cooking temperature. The whistle sounds when the pressure regulator releases extra steam and is indicative of how long the contents have been cooking. Remember, never try and force open the lid. Allow the cooker to cool a little or release the pressure gently by lifting the valve and wait till the lid slides open easily.

'Tava'

This heavy, slightly concave, rimless skillet is used to cook the unleavened flatbreads typical of this region. I have always preferred the puffy, evenly cooked breads from the traditional, cast-iron 'tava', but more light-weight, and even non-stick 'tavas' are gradually gaining popularity.

'Tadka' Pan/Spoon

When 'tadka' is infused at the end of the cooking process, the utensil used is usually a small, heavy pan or a special long-handled ladle, ideally made of iron. The heavy utensil heats the 'ghee' or oil evenly, allowing the spices and other 'tadka' ingredients to brown without charring them.

CONVERSION OF MEASURES

1 cup = 128 gm or 4.5 oz or 240 ml
1 tbsp =15 gm
1 tsp = 5 gm
½ tsp = 2.5 gm
¼ tsp = 1.5 gm

APPROXIMATE WEIGHT

Small potato = 50–80 gm
Medium potato = 80–100 gm
Large potato = 180–200 gm
Small onion = 50–60 gm
Medium onion = 70–80 gm
Large onion = 140–150 gm
Small tomato = 50–60 gm
Medium tomato = 80–90 gm
Large tomato = 120 gm

All recipes in this book serve six.

□

TIPANO (Sindhi Calendar)

The Sindhi and the Hindu calendars, both follow the lunar year as opposed to the solar year. A lunar month is the time the Moon takes to revolve around the Earth, approximately 29.5 days. A year is 12 full cycles of the phases of the moon—approximately 354 days. A solar year is measured by the time Earth takes to complete one full orbit of the Sun—a little more than 365 days. It is this difference of 11 days that explains the difference of dates between the two calendars.

Given below is a list of festivals that are celebrated by the Sindhi community and when they fall. As you go through the book, you will find some festivals have been elaborated. This is because I wanted it to be a gentle reminder of a particular dish being associated with its celebration. It is so easy for these traditions to be forgotten or overlooked.

Chet/ Vesakh	March /April	Nandda Ekanna; Cheti Chand
Vesakh/Jeth	April/May	Akshaya Tithi (Akhand Teej)
Jeth/Aakhar	May/June	Nirjal Ekadasi; Yogini Ekadasi
Aakhar/Sawan	June/July	Chaaliyo; Ann-Matyo
Sawan/Bhado	July/August	Gogo; Chaumasa Teejri; Vaddi Thhadri
Bhado/Assoo	August/September	Mahalaxshmi jo Sagro; Shraadh
Assoo/Katti	September/October	Vadda Ekaanna; Dussehra; Sharad Poornima
Katti/Manghir	October/November	Katti jo Mahino; Diyaari; Vaddi Gyaras; Guru Nanak Jayanti
Manghir/Poh	November/December	
Poh/Mangh	December/January	Tirmuri; Lal Loi
Mangh/Faag	January/February	Basant Panchami; Maha Shivratri
Faag/Chet	February/ March	Holi; Dhuryo

Festivals

Cheti Chand (Recipe: Kara Channa)

The Sindhi New Year marks the birth anniversary of Ishtadev Uderolal Jhulelal (Jhoolelal), who is considered by the Sindhis to be the reincarnation of Lord Varuna, the God of Rivers and water is a primary deity for the community. Not only was their homeland situated on the banks of the Indus, but for centuries, Sindhi merchants have been traversing through waters, carrying their cargo to distant lands. Jhulelal tikanas (temples) across the country hold huge celebrations to mark this day with tayhri and dry channa being the main food shared.

Akshaya Tithi (Akhand Teej)

Dedicated to Lord Vishnu, offering prayers to him on this day is an opportunity to eradicate one's sins and sorrows. Also, performing rituals to honour one's ancestors on this day will, it is believed, ensure endless good fortune, health, wealth and love. Akshaya tithi is associated with abundance—the word 'akshaya' itself means 'never diminishing'.

Ann-Matyo

From this day, in the month of Sawan, traditionally the cereals consumed for the main meal would change: instead of the wheat and rice, chapatis made of gram flour are eaten. This was to suit the metabolic needs of the body to the external changes in the environment—that is to say, the weather conditions brought on by the change in season.

Vaddi Thhadri (Recipe: Moonganji Dhotal Dal)

'Thadri', which means 'thadho' or cold, is celebrated to honour Jog Maya Devi, the sister of Lord Krishna. The Devi, an aspect of Goddess Durga, is also known as Sitala Ma, who manifests when enraged in the form of measles, chicken pox, small pox and 'heat related' diseases. So, on this day from dawn to dawn, no fires are lit at all to appease the Devi. Only cold food, cooked the previous day, including lolo, besan koki, moongdal phulka, bhindi, karela are consumed and offered.

Shraadh

The month of September, Bhado, is meant to honour ancestors, to perform 'shraadh'—offer food and prayers for the solace of the deceased's soul.

Sharad Poornima (Recipe: Khumb)

The full moon of the month of Assoo is believed to be highly potent and beneficial—its rays have the power to heal. For this reason, a bowl of kheerni, or rice pudding, is left in the moonlight to be blessed and then consumed the next morning to ensure well-being.

Katti Jo Mahino

Katti is considered an immensely auspicious month during which is celebrated Diyaari or Deepavali, which marks the return of Lord Rama to his kingdom of Ayodhya. Dhanteras starts off the celebrations, followed by Nandde Diyaari, or Chhoti Deepavali, marks the day Lord Krishna killed the demon Narakasur. Then comes Diyaari itself during which prayers are offered to Goddess Mahalaxshmi, the provider of wealth and good fortune. Govardhan Puja or Annakut is the next day to honour Mother Earth, the provider of sustenance.

Tirmuri and Lal Loi

Tirmuri marks the onset the harvesting season with the sun's transition to the Northern Hemisphere. One of the few festivals that is based on the solar calendar and falls on the same day each year, is the Sindhi equivalent of Makar Sankranti, which is celebrated in several parts of India on 14 January, coinciding with the winter solstice. Lal Loi on the evening before Tirmuri, is celebrated with a bonfire, while kite-flying marks Tirmuri day. Moori (radish) and sesame-seed sweets, such as til laddu, are very popular on this harvest festival.

Holi

The bonfire on the eve of Holi, which symbolises the burning of the demon Holika, marks the beginning of the celebrations. The next morning sees the splashing of colours and the showering of flower petals in an expression of unbounded joy that marks the change of season. It is, of course, a huge favourite with children and is accompanied by feasting on sweets and savouries. It is one of the few festivals where non-vegetarian food is served. Most of the sweets and savouries served, such as 'geeyar', samosa stuffed with Karachi halwa, are elaborate preparations that are made by a professional 'halwai' (confectioner).

□

ACKNOWLEDGEMENTS

For their enthusiastic appreciation of my cooking and their constant, unfailing support in every aspect of my life, I would like to express my deepest gratitude to my family:

Jayant Advani, Ameera Sushil Shah, Geetika Advani, Hemant Sachdev and though last, but never the least, my husband, Sudesh Sachdev.

This book may not have seen the light of day if it were not for the inspiration and encouragement I received from:

Gayatri Goswami, Neha Verma, Ritu Handa, Razia Grover, Serena Chopra and Sunita Gihani.

My sincere thanks to each one of them and profound gratitude.

My appreciation to Madhu Madhavi Singh for putting her heart into editing this book.

CONTENTS

SAAG

LEGUMES & LENTILS

MEAT & CHICKEN

ROTIS

BIRYANIS

CONDIMENTS—CHUTNEY, ACHAR, MURBA

DESSERTS

BASIC MASALAS

Bhugal Masalo
(Bhuna Masala)

Ingredients

Onion (medium)	4	finely chopped
Tomatoes (medium)	6	chopped
Green chillies	6	chopped
Ginger	1½ -inch piece	chopped
Oil	½ cup	

Method

Heat oil in a *kadhai* on medium flame.

Saute onions till golden brown, then remove from oil and set aside.

Remove *kadhai* from heat but leave oil in it.

Grind tomatoes, green chillies and ginger together, add fried onions and grind again to make a fine paste.

Heat the *kadhai* again, pour in the paste and cook, stirring briskly to avoid it sticking to the *kadhai* and burning.

When the masala thickens, changes colour to a golden brown and starts leaving oil at the edges, remove from heat.

Leave to cool, then transfer to an airtight container.

If refrigerated, use within four to five days.

If frozen it can be stored for up to 15 days.

To use

If frozen, make sure the masala has de-frozen completely or it will splatter in hot oil.

Heat a little oil in a pan, add masala and choice of vegetables.

Add water to lighten masala paste into a thick gravy.

Cover and leave to cook on a low flame. Stir occasionally.

When vegetables are cooked, take off flame, garnish and serve.

□

Alo Savo Masalo
(Wet Green Masala)

Ingredients

Fresh coriander	1½ cup	chopped
Garlic	20–24 cloves	
Green chillies	5	chopped
Turmeric powder	1 tbsp	
Coriander powder	1 tbsp	
Raw mango powder	½ tbsp	
Salt	to taste	

Method

Grind the garlic and chillies coarsely.
Add coriander and grind again but keep paste coarse.
Add all the dry spices and mix well.
Transfer to an airtight container.
If refrigerated use within four to five days.
If frozen it can be stored for up to 15 days.

To use

If frozen, make sure the masala has thawed completely or it will splutter in hot oil.

Heat a little oil in a pan, add green masala and choice of vegetables.

Add water to lighten masala paste into a thick gravy.

Cover and leave to cook on a low flame. Stir occasionally.

When vegetables are cooked, take off flame add a dash of lemon juice and serve.

□

Bhugal Masalo (Bhuna Masala) • *P-35*

Alo Savo Masalo (Wet Green Masala) • *P-36*

Garam Masalo (Mixed Hot Spices) • P-37

Kunnewara Bheeh (Spicy Lotus Stem Tossed in a Clay Pot) • P-38

Garam Masalo

(Mixed Hot Spices)

Ingredients

Cumin	½ cup
Black peppercorns	½ cup
Cloves	¼ cup
Bay leaves	6
Cinnamon	½ cup
Star aniseed	6–7
Mace	1 tbsp
Nutmeg	1
Green cardamom	15–20
Black cardamom	6–7

Method

Sun-dry all ingredients.
Grind into fine powder and store in an airtight jar.
Use as indicated in recipe.

□

SNACKS

Kunnewara Bheeh

(Spicy Lotus stem tossed in a Clay Pot)

Ingredients

Lotus stem (thick)	750 gm	peeled and cut into 2-inch pieces
Green chillies	3	finely chopped
Garlic	4–5	finely chopped
Red chilli powder	¾ tsp	
Cinnamon	¾ tsp	
Black pepper	¾ tsp	
Garam masala	¾ tsp	
Salt	to taste	

To garnish

Spring garlic	½ cup	finely chopped

Method

Pressure-cook lotus stem pieces in water till cooked (about two whistles). Drain water, and transfer to a clay pot (kunne, matka).

Add chillies, garlic, chilli powder, cinnamon, black pepper and garam masala.

Cover and toss to mix thoroughly and garnish.

Serving tip

Perfect with green chutney on the side.

□

Bheehanja Pakora
(Lotus stem Fritters)

Ingredients

Lotus stem	500 gm	peeled and cut into 2-inch pieces
Fresh coriander	½ cup	leaves
Fresh mint	½ cup	leaves
Green chillies	2	
Lemon juice	3 tbsp	
Gram flour	½ cup	
Coriander powder	½ tsp	
Red chilli powder	½ tsp	
Carom	½ tsp	
Salt	to taste	

To cook

Water	as needed
Mustard oil	to deep fry

Method

Pressure-cook the lotus stems for two whistles in lightly salted water.

Grind the fresh coriander, mint and green chillies into a paste. Add salt and lemon juice.

Remove cooked lotus stems from the cooker and drain.

Slit each piece lengthwise down on one side, stuff with coriander paste and set aside.

In a bowl, mix gram flour dry spices, salt and water, then whisk briskly to form a thick, smooth batter.

Heat oil in a *kadhai*, then lower flame to medium.

Dip lotus stem in batter, drop into heated oil and fry till golden brown.

Serving tip

Best served hot with ketchup.

□

Dahi-Wada
(Lentil dumplings in curd)

Ingredients

Black gram dal	1 cup
Yellow lentil dal	¼ cup
Green chilli	1
Ginger	1-inch piece
Asafoetida	a p-inch
Cumin seeds	1 tsp
Fresh coriander	¼ cup
Black peppercorn	9–10
Salt	to taste
Curd	2 cups

To cook

Oil	to deep fry

To garnish

Red chilli powder	1 tsp
Roasted cumin powder	1 tsp
Sweet tamarind chutney	1 tbsp

Method

Soak both dals for overnight, wash and drain.

Put in a blender, add green chilli, asafoetida and ginger and grind into thick batter.

Transfer batter to a bowl, add salt, cumin and coriander leaves, black peppercorn and beat continuously in one direction till fluffy.

Heat oil in *kadhai.*

Drop batter into the hot oil, one spoonful at a time to form dumplings and fry till golden brown.

Remove from oil and soak in water for about 15 minutes.

Add salt to the curd and whip to a smooth, creamy consistency. Add a little water if it is too thick.

Gently squeeze water from dumplings one at a time and put into curd.

Garnish and serve.

□

Dal-Chhola-Dhabal

(Bun & Chickpeas)

Ingredients		
Chickpeas	1 cup	
Bengal gram dal	1 cup	
Onion (medium)	1	finely chopped
Green chillies	2	finely chopped
Ginger	1-inch piece	grated
Tamarind	¼ cup	
Plain buns	6	
Dry spices		
Cumin seeds	1 tsp	
Red chilli powder	1 tbsp	
Coriander powder	1 tbsp	
Salt	to taste	
To cook		
Water	2½ cups	
Oil		
To garnish		
Onion (medium)	1	finely chopped
Garam masala	1 tsp	
Fresh coriander leaves		

Method

Soak chickpeas and Bengal gram dal overnight.

Pressure-cook chickpeas in salted water for four whistles till soft. Allow to cool, drain and set aside.

Pressure cook dal for one whistle. Allow to cool, drain and set aside.

Heat oil in kadai, add cumin seeds, onion, green chillies, ginger, red chilli powder, coriander powder and salt.

Bheehanja Pakora (Lotus Stem Fritters) • P-39

Dahi-Wada (Lentil Dumplings in Curd) • P-40

Kara Channa (Black Gram) • P-44

Sindhi Tikki (Sindhi Cutlets) • P-45

Saute for two minutes, then add two cups water, chickpeas and dal.

After boiling simmer for five minutes until thick.

Soak tamarind in ½ cup hot water, then mash into pulp, add salt, red chilli powder and strain.

Slice pao horizontally into two and lay flat on platter.

Spread tamarind water and top with cooked chickpeas.

Garnish and serve.

Serving tip

Green chutney on the side works well.

□

Kara Channa
(Black gram)

Ingredients

Black gram	1 cup	
Cumin	1 tbsp	
Asafoetida	a pinch	
Dry red chilli	1-2	whole
Garam masala	1 tbsp	
Coriander powder	1 tbsp	

To cook

Oil	2 tbsp	

To garnish

Onion (small)	1	finely chopped
Lemon juice	1 tbsp	
Fresh coriander leaves		

Method

Soak black gram overnight.

Pressure-cook in mildly salted water for three to four whistles. Allow to cool and drain.

Heat oil in a pan, add cumin, asafoetida and stir well.

Add garam masala and coriander powder and mix well.

Garnish and serve.

□

Sindhi Tikki

(Sindhi Cutlets)

Ingredients

Potatoes (medium)	4–5	
Bengal gram	2 tbs	
Green chillies	2	finely chopped
Cumin	½ tsp	
Asafoetida	a p-inch	
Coriander powder	1 tsp	
Red chilli powder	1 tsp	
Raw mango powder	1 tsp	
Chaat masala	1 tsp	
Garam masala	1 tsp	
Salt	to taste	

To cook

Oil	to shallow fry

Method

Soak Bengal gram for about two hours and then boil, drain and set aside.

Boil the potatoes, peel, add salt and mash into a smooth dough.

Heat oil in a *kadhai*, add cumin seeds, asafoetida, other dry masalas, green chillies and dal. Saute and set aside.

Take a little potato dough and roll it into a small ball.

Flatten, place Bengal gram mixture in the centre and roll again.

Gently flatten once more to make cutlets.

Heat oil in a tava on a low flame and shallow fry cutlets on both sides till golden brown and crisp.

Serving tip

Best with green chutney on the side.

□

VEGETABLES

Sai Bhaji
(Mixed Vegetables)

Ingredients

Spinach	3 cups	finely chopped
Onion (medium)	1½	finely chopped
Green chillies	3	finely chopped
Tomatoes	3	cut in small pieces
Bengal gram dal	½ cup	
Potato (small)	2	cut in ½ -inch pieces
Okra	4	cut in small pieces
French beans	4	cut in small pieces
Turmeric powder	½ tsp	
Salt	to taste	

To cook

Oil	1½ tbsp
Water	1½ cup

For tadka

Ghee	4 tsp	
Ginger	½ tsp	grated
Garlic	5–6 cloves	chopped
Coriander powder	½ tsp	
Red chilli powder	½ tsp	
Raw mango powder	½ tsp	

Method

Heat the oil in a pressure cooker pan, add onions, green chillies and cook lightly.

Add tomatoes, spinach and Bengal gram and then saute for one minute.

Sai Bhaji (Mixed Vegetables) • P-46

Kathal (Jackfruit) • P-48

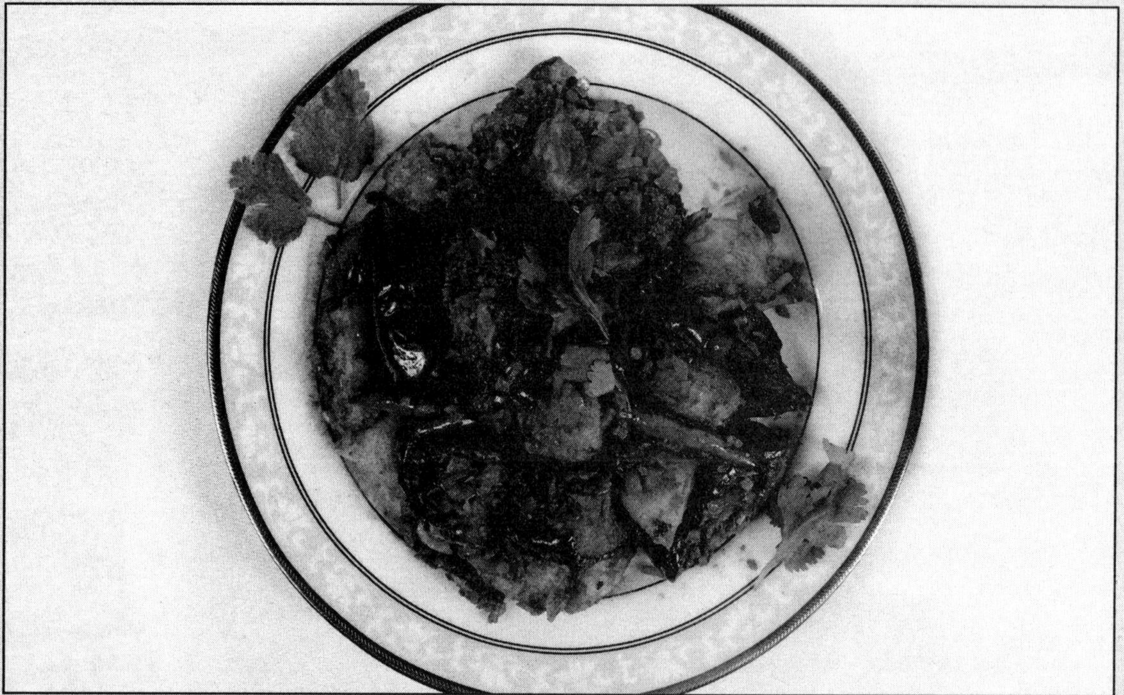

Patata–Vangan (Potato & Brinjal) • *P-49*

Bheendyun-Meha-Patata (Okra, Indian Squash & Potato) • *P-50*

Add potatoes, okra, French beans and stir lightly.

Add salt, turmeric and water.

Close lid and pressure-cook for three to four whistles.

Allow to cool slightly, then open the cooker and coarsely mash the spinach mix.

Tadka

Heat ghee in a tadka pan.

Add ginger, garlic and dry spices.

Allow to brown slightly, then drown in spinach mix and cover instantly.

Serving tip

Goes well with khichri or onion pulao.

□

Kathal
(Jackfruit)

Ingredients

Jackfruit	2 cups	chopped into approximately 1-inch cubes
Onions (large)	4	finely chopped
Tomato (large)	2	chopped
Green chillies	2	finely chopped
Turmeric powder	1 tsp	
Coriander power	1 tsp	
Red chilli powder	1 tsp	
Raw mango powder	1½ tsp	
Salt	to taste	

To cook

Oil	1¾ cup
Water	1½ cup

To garnish

Fresh coriander	leaves

Method

Wash jackfruit and rub with salt.
Heat 1½ cup oil in a *kadhai* and deep fry jackfruit till golden, drain and set aside.
Heat 2 tbsp oil in pressure cooker pan.
Add jackfruit and onions, then saute for 2–3 minutes till slightly brown.
Add tomatoes, chillies and dry spices and stir well.
Add water, close lid and pressure-cook for two whistles.
Allow to cool, open and stir lightly.
Garnish with fresh coriander and serve.

□

Patata-Vangan

(Potato & Brinjal)

Ingredients

Potatoes (medium)	3	cut into small pieces
Brinjal (round, large)	2	cut into small pieces
Onions (large)	3	finely chopped
Tomato (medium)	2	chopped
Green chillies	3	finely chopped
Turmeric powder	½ tsp	
Coriander powder	1 tsp	
Red chilli powder	1tsp	
Raw mango powder	1 tsp	
Salt	to taste	

To cook

Mustard oil	6 tbsp

To garnish

Garam masala	1 tsp
Fresh coriander	leaves

Method

Heat the oil in a *kadhai*.
Add potatoes and saute for two minutes.
Add brinjal, onion, tomatoes, green chillies, turmeric and salt.
Cover the *kadhai* and leave to cook for 5 minutes.
Add remaining dry spices and stir well.
Sprinkle garam masala, garnish with fresh coriander and serve.

□

Bheendyun-Meha-Patata

(Okra, Indian squash & Potato)

Ingredients

Okra	250 gm	
Indian squash (medium)	6	
Potatoes (medium)	3	
Green masala	6 tbsp	
Green chilli	2	finely chopped
Turmeric powder	1½ tbsp	
Coriander powder	1½ tbsp	
Raw mango powder	1½ tbsp	
Salt	taste	

To cook

Mustard oil	4–5 tbsp
Water	3 cups

To garnish

Fresh coriander leaves

Method

Carefully slit okra along one length to create a pocket and set aside.
Slice Indian squash and potatoes into thick circles and set aside.
Spoon green masala into a bowl, add dry spices and mix well.
Gently stuff the okra with this masala.
Coat Indian squash, potato slices with any leftover masala.
Heat oil in *kadhai*, place okra, Indian squash and potatoes separately.
Add water and cover.
Turn flame down to medium and leave to cook for 20–25 minutes.
Remove cover and check that the vegetables are cooked.
Garnish with fresh coriander and serve.

□

Sindhi Karhi

Ingredients

Gram flour	¾ cup	
Okra	100 gm	
Indian squash	100 gm	cut into 1-inch pieces
Potatoes (medium)	2	cut into 1-inch pieces
Cluster beans	50 gm	cut into 1-inch pieces
Peas	50 gm	
Lotus stem	50 gm	cut into -inch pieces
Green chillies	4–5	finely chopped
Tamarind	½ cup	pulped
Cumin	1 tsp	
Fenugreek	1 tsp	
Asafoetida	1 p-inch	
Salt	to taste	
Turmeric powder	1 tsp	
Red chilli powder	1 tsp	

To cook

Mustard oil	½ cup	
Water	8 cups	boiling

For tadka

Mustard oil	3 tbsp
Whole, dry red chillies	2–4
Coriander powder	1 tsp
Karhi leaves	3–4 sprigs

Method

Carefully slit okra vertically down one side, deep fry and set aside.

Boil lotus stem and set aside.

Heat oil in pan, add gram flour and roast till aromatic, then add cumin, fenugreek and asafoetida.

Continue roasting on medium heat for about five minutes.

Add boiling water, salt and turmeric powder and keep stirring till the Karhi starts boiling.

Simmer and add potatoes, Indian squash, peas, cluster beans, and lotus stem.

When these vegetables are cooked, add the fried okra and green chillies.

Simmer for two minutes and add tamarind pulp.

Tadka

Heat oil in tadka pan, add mustard seeds, when they start to splutter.

Add whole red chillies, coriander powder, and then the Karhi leaves.

Drown in Karhi and cover instantly.

Serving tip

Makes a complete meal when served with rice.

☐

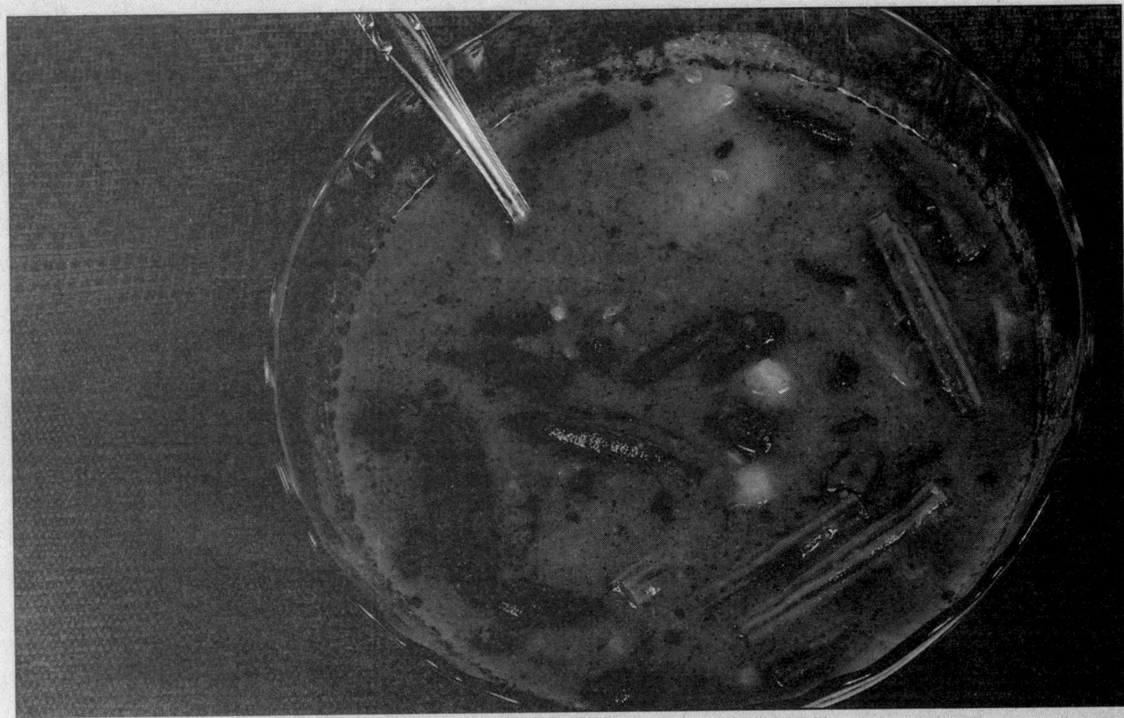

Sindhi Karhi • P-51

Paneer-Simla Mirch (Cottage Cheese & Capsicum) • P-54

Tuk (Crispy Fried Potato)

Tuk
(Crispy Fried Potato)

Ingredients

Potatoes (medium)	12
Coriander powder	1½ tsp
Red chilli powder	1½ tsp
Raw mango powder	1½ tsp
Salt	to taste

To cook

Oil	to deep fry

Method

Boil potatoes till cooked but not soft. Cool, peel, cut in half and slits in them with a knife.

Heat oil in *kadhai* and deep fry potatoes on medium heat till crisp and pale gold in colour.

Remove from oil.

Allow to cool completely, then fry again till golden brown in colour.

Remove from oil, sprinkle with dry spices, toss to mix well and serve hot.

Do not cover for it will become soggy.

□

Paneer-Simla Mirch
(Cottage Cheese & Capsicum)

Ingredients

Paneer	¾ cup	cut into pieces about 2-inch long
Capsicum (medium)	3	cut into pieces about 2-inch long
Tomatoes (large)	3	
Green chillies	3	
Ginger	1 tbsp	grated
Turmeric powder	¾ tsp	
Coriander powder	¾ tsp	
Red chilli powder	¾ tsp	
Salt	to taste	

To cook

Mustard oil	4–5 tbsp
Water	2 cup

To garnish

Garam masala	¾ tsp

Method

Grind tomatoes, green chillies and ginger into a coarse paste.
Heat oil in pan, add paste and fry.
Add dry spices, then paneer and capsicum.
Stir well, add water, cover and leave on medium flame.
When cooked, sprinkle with garam masala and serve.

□

Besan Tikki Bhajji

(Gram-flour Dumplings in Gravy)

Ingredients

FOR TIKKI

Gram flour	1 cup	
Green chillies	2	finely chopped
Onion small	1	finely chopped
Oil	2 tbsp	
Coriander powder	½ tsp	
Red chilli powder	½ tsp	
Whole coriander seeds	½ tsp	
Pomegranate powder	½ tsp	
Salt	to taste	
Water	to form dough	lukewarm

FOR GRAVY

Onion (medium)	3–4	chopped
Tomato (large)	1	chopped
Green chillies	2	finely chopped
Turmeric powder	½ tsp	
Coriander powder	½ tsp	
Red chilli powder	½ tsp	
Raw mango powder	½ tsp	
Salt	to taste	

To cook

Oil—for tikkis	to deep fry
for gravy	2–3 tsp
Water	1 cup

Coriander leaves for garnishing

Method

TIKKIS

Mix all ingredients except water in a bowl. The mixture should bind to form a crumbly ball when pressed inside your palm.

Add small amounts of water to knead mix into a tight dough.

Divide dough into 10–12 pieces, roll into tight balls in your palm and flatten slightly to form tikkis.

Heat oil in *kadhai* and deep fry till golden brown and set aside.

GRAVY

Heat 2–3 tsp oil in *kadhai*, add onion, tomato, green chillies and saute.

Add dry spices and mix well.

Add tikkis, stir, then add water.

Cover and cook on low flame for 25–30 minutes, garnish with fresh coriander leaves.

Serving tip

Goes well with rotis.

□

Besan Tikki Bhajji (Gram-flour Dumplings in Gravy) • P-55

Dhingri (Dry Mushrooms) • P-58

Vari-Patata (Wadi-Potato) • P-60

Bharyal Karela (Stuffed Bitter Gourd) • P-62

Dahi Wara Meha

(Indian Squash in Mustard Curd)

Ingredients

Indian squash (medium)	12	peeled and cut into 4
Mustard seeds	1½ tsp	
Garlic cloves	12	chopped
Tomato (large)	1	chopped
Green chillies	3	
Turmeric powder	1½ tsp	
Coriander powder	¾ tsp	
Red chilli powder	1½ tsp	
Salt	to taste	
Curd	1½ cup	lightly whisked till smooth

To cook

Oil	4–5 tbsp
Water	1 cup

Method

Heat oil in pressure cooker pan, add mustard seeds.
When seeds start to splutter, add garlic and saute till golden brown.
Add tomatoes and green chillies, and half-cup water.
Close lid and pressure-cook for two whistles.
Take off heat, allow to cool and open and return to heat.
Add Indian squash, remaining dry spices and water.
Stir well, close cooker and leave on medium flame for two whistles.
Take off heat, allow to cool and open.
Add curd and mix well (add a little hot water to increase gravy if desired).

Serving tip

Goes well with rotis.

□

Dhingri
(Dry Mushrooms)

Ingredients

Dhingri	1½ cup	small pieces
Onion (medium)	3	finely chopped
Green chillies	3–4	chopped
Cumin	¾ tsp	
Garlic	4 cloves	chopped
Tomatoes (medium)	3	chopped
Cinnamon	1½ -inch stick	
Bay leaves	2	
Cloves	2–3	
Turmeric powder	¾ tsp	
Coriander powder	¾ tsp	
Red chilli powder	¾ tsp	

To cook

Mustard oil	4 tbsp
Water	1½ cup

To garnish

Garam masala	3/4 tsp
Fresh coriander leaves	

Method

Wash dhingri thoroughly as it usually has a lot of dry mud; soak overnight.

Heat oil in pressure cooker, add onion, green chillies, cumin, garlic and saute.

Add tomatoes, cinnamon, bay leaves, cloves, and cook till tomatoes are half cooked.

Add enough water to make a thick gravy, add remaining dry spices and stir.

Add dhingri and mix well.

Add remaining water, close lid and pressure-cook for two whistles.

Allow to cool, open and transfer to serving dish.

Garnish with garam masala and coriander leaves.

Serving tip
Goes well with rotis.

□

Vari-Patata
(Wadi-Potato)

Ingredients

Vari (small, black gram)	1½ cup	
Potatoes (medium)	3	chopped
Onion (medium)	3	chopped
Tomatoes	3	chopped
Green chillies	3–4	chopped
Cinnamon	1-inch stick	
Bay leaves	2	
Cumin	1½ tsp	
Turmeric powder	¾ tsp	
Coriander powder	¾ tsp	
Red chilli powder	¾ tsp	
Salt	to taste	

To cook

Oil	4½ tbsp
Water	2½ cup

To garnish

Garam masala	¾ tsp
Raw mango powder	¾ tsp
Fresh coriander leaves	

Method

Heat oil in pressure cooker, saute onions, then add green chillies and tomatoes.

When tomatoes are cooked, add a little water, wait till it boils and turn heat to low.

Add dry masalas, vari, potatoes stir well and cook for two minutes and then add remaining water.

Close lid and pressure-cook for two whistles. Allow to cool, open and transfer to serving dish.

Sprinkle with garam masala and mango powder and garnish with coriander leaves.

Options

Sometimes, for a change, I substitute potatoes with lotus stem or Indian squash.

□

Bharyal Karela
(Stuffed Bitter Gourd)

Ingredients

Bitter gourd	12
Mango powder	1 tbsp
Mango pickle masala	3 tbsp
Salt	to taste

To cook

Mustard oil	5 tbsp

Method

Scrape the skin off the bitter gourd, rub with salt and set aside for an hour.

Slit bitter gourd lengthwise down one side to create a pocket.

Thoroughly rub bitter gourd with salt both inside and outside, and set aside for an hour.

Then gently squeeze bitter gourd and skin to remove excess salt and bitter juice.

Wash three to four times in water and set aside.

Heat oil in pan, add bitter gourd skin, dry ingredients and saute. Remove from heat.

Divide sauteed masala equally and stuff into each bitter gourd.

Brush bitter gourd with oil; place on grill tray and grill till golden brown.

□

Sindhi Patata
(Sindhi Potatoes)

Ingredients

Potatoes (medium)	12	cut into thin slices
Turmeric powder	1½ tsp	
Coriander powder	1½ tsp	
Raw mango powder	1½ tsp	
Red chilli powder	¾ tsp	
Black pepper powder	¾ tsp	
Salt	to taste	

To cook

Mustard oil	4 tbsp

Method

Heat oil in a *kadhai* and add potatoes.

Add turmeric and salt, stir well and cover. Put a weight on the lid to maintain the steam inside.

When potatoes are half-cooked, add remaining dry spices and mix well.

Cover and cook for 10 minutes more.

Serving tip

Goes well with rotis or pooris.

□

Bharyal Tooriyun
(Stuffed Ridge Gourd)

Ingredients

Ridge gourd (medium)	8	
Green chillies	2	finely chopped
Garlic cloves	5–6	crushed
Turmeric powder	½ tsp	
Coriander powder	½ tsp	
Red chilli powder	½ tsp	
Raw mango powder	½ tsp	
Salt	to taste	

To cook

Mustard oil	2 tbsp

Method

Peel ridge gourd and slit lengthwise on one side to create a pocket.

Mix green chillies, garlic, the dry spices and salt, and lightly stuff the ridge gourd.

Heat oil in a flat pan and lay out the ridge gourd to cook on a medium flame.

The ridge gourd will leave water, turn gently and cook till dry.

□

Sindhi Patata (Sindhi Potatoes) • *P-63*

Bharyal Tooriyun (Stuffed Ridge Gourd) • *P-64*

Vangan Bharto (Mashed Brinjal) • P-65

Sai Thoom Patata (Potatoes & Spring Garlic) • P-67

Vangan Bharto
(Mashed Brinjal)

Ingredients

Brinjal (round, medium)	3	
Onion (medium)	1½	finely chopped
Green chillies	3	finely chopped
Raw mango (medium)	1½	peeled and grated
Coriander powder	1½ tsp	
Salt	to taste	

To cook

Mustard oil	4½ tbsp

Method

Roast brinjal over an open flame until the skin bursts and turns black.

Allow to cool, peel skin and mash the brinjal.

Add onion and green chillies, and raw mango.

Heat oil in a pan, add mashed mixture and cook till soft.

Serving tip

Goes well with roti or poori.

□

Vangan-Basar

(Brinjal & Onions)

Ingredients

Brinjal (round, medium)	2	
Onions (medium)	3–4	chopped
Green chilli	3	finely chopped
Tomato (large)	1	chopped
Turmeric powder	½ tbsp	
Coriander powder	1 tbsp	
Raw mango powder	1 tbsp	
Red chilli	1 tbsp	
Salt	to taste	

To cook

Mustard oil	½ cup

To garnish

Garam masala	½ tsp
Fresh coriander leaves	

Method

Cut brinjal lengthwise into four parts and then slits in each piece with a knife.

Rub with salt and set aside to marinade for half an hour, then wash well.

Heat oil in a *kadhai* and fry the brinjal pieces lightly, till golden. Take out and leave to cool.

In *kadhai*, add onion and green chilli. Cook for a minute, then add tomatoes, and dry masalas. Stir well and cook for two minutes.

Take out half the masala and place the brinjal in the *kadhai*, onions with masala and coriander leaves.

Cover with the masala you had taken out.

Cover *kadhai* and leave to cook on low heat, without stirring, for five minutes.

Gently place on serving dish, garnish and serve.

□

Sai Thoom Patata
(Potatoes & Spring Garlic)

Ingredients

Spring garlic	2 cups	finely chopped
Potatoes (medium)	4	cut into 8 pieces
Tomato (medium)	2	cut into 8 pieces
Green chillies	3	finely chopped
Ginger	1½ tsp	grated
Turmeric powder	¾ tsp	
Coriander powder	1½ tsp	
Red chilli powder	¾ tsp	
Raw mango powder	1½ tsp	
Salt	to taste	

To cook

Mustard oil	4½ tbsp

Method

Heat oil in *kadhai*, Add ginger, green chillies, tomatoes, potatoes and spring garlic.

Sprinkle dry spices and stir well.

Cover and cook on low flame for 15–20 minutes, stirring occasionally.

Check that potatoes are cooked, take off heat and serve.

Serving tip

Goes well with rotis.

□

Bheeh-Patata
(Lotus Stem & Potatoes)

Ingredients

Lotus stems	250 gm	cut diagonally
Potatoes (medium)	3	cut in long pieces
Onions (medium)	3	finely chopped
Tomato (large)	1½	chopped
Green chillies	2	finely chopped
Ginger	1½ tsp	grated
Turmeric powder	¾ tsp	
Coriander powder	2 tbsp	
Red chilli powder	½ tsp	
Cinnamon	1-inch stick	
Salt	to taste	

To cook

Water	2½ cup
Mustard oil	4–5 tbsp

To garnish

Garam masala	3/4 tsp

Method

Pressure-cook lotus stems in a cup of salted water for two whistles. Take out, drain and set aside.

Heat oil in pressure cooker pan, add onions and saute till golden brown.

Add ginger, green chillies, tomatoes and ½ cup water, close lid and pressure-cook for two whistles.

Allow to cool, then open and lightly mash onion, tomato and chilli mix.

Add lotus stems, potatoes, dry spices and cook for two minutes.

Then add 1 cup water, close lid again and pressure-cook for one whistle.

Allow to cool before opening. Transfer to serving dish and garnish with garam masala.

Serving tip

Goes well with roti or onion pulao.

□

Raswara Karela-Patata
(Bitter Gourd Potatoes)

Ingredients

Bitter gourd (small)	15–20	
Potatoes (medium)	2	cut into small pieces
Garlic	20–24 cloves	
Green chillies	3	finely chopped
Turmeric powder	1 tsp	
Coriander powder	1 tsp	
Red chilli powder	½ tsp	
Salt	to taste	

To cook

Oil	2–3 tbsp
Water	2½ cups

To garnish

Raw mango powder	1 tbsp
Garam masala	1tsp
Fresh coriander leaves	

Method

Peel bitter gourd and carefully slit lengthwise on one side to create a pocket.

Gently rub salt both inside and out and set aside for one hour.

Heat oil in pressure cooker pan, add garlic and saute till light brown.

Then add ½ cup water and pressure-cook for one whistle.

Allow to cool then open. Add potatoes, green chillies, dry spices, two cups of water and pressure-cook for two whistles.

Wash and squeeze-dry bitter gourd, then shallow fry in pan till golden brown.

Place in serving bowl and pour cooked potatoes on top.

Garnish with mango powder, garam masala and fresh coriander leaves.

Serving tip

Goes well with rotis.

☐

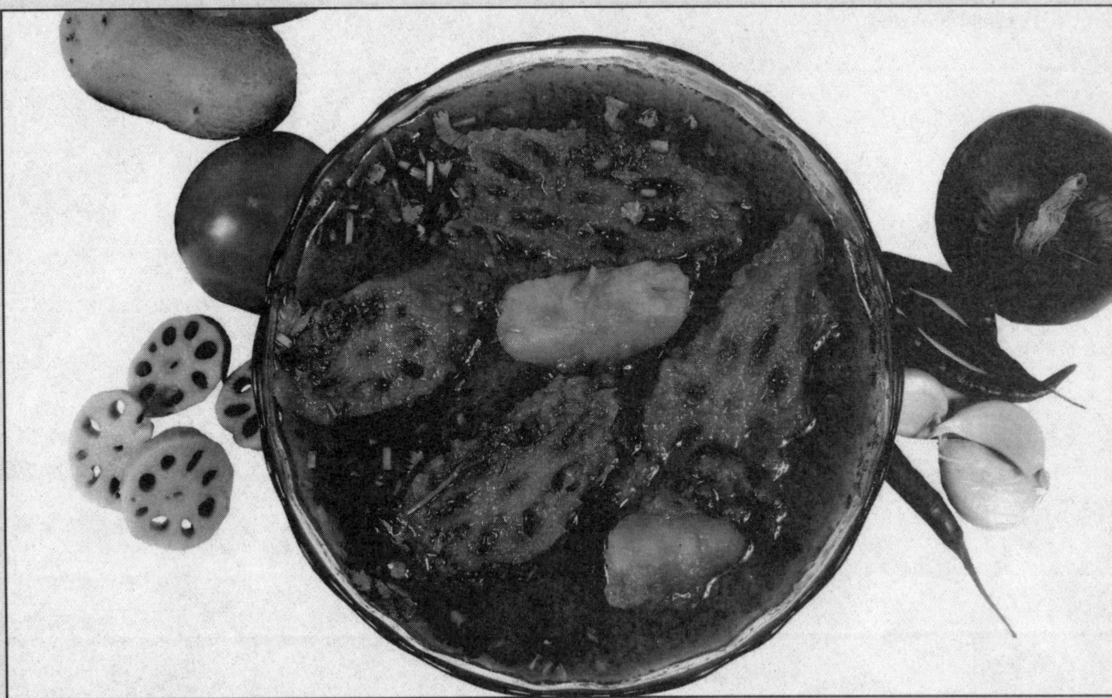

Bheeh–Patata (Lotus Stem & Potatoes) • *P-68*

Raswara Karela-Patata (Bitter Gourd Potatoes) • *P-70*

Seyal Phulka (Roti in Green Masala) • P-71

Raswara Methi-Patata (Fenugreek Potatoes) • P-72

Seyal Phulka
(Roti in Green Masala)

Ingredients

Wheat flour	1 cup	
Water	2 cups	
Coriander leaves	¾ cup	chopped
Green chillies	3–4	
Garlic	12–14 cloves	
Turmeric powder	1 tsp	
Coriander powder	1 tsp	
Raw mango powder	1 tsp	
Salt	to taste	

To cook

Oil	4 tbsp
Water	1½ cups

Method

Knead wheat flour to a soft dough with water.

Divide dough into 8 and roll each piece into a ball.

Take one ball, press flat and use a rolling pin to roll out into a thin, flat, 5-inch circle (approx.).

Place on heated tava and cook on both sides.

When all eight phulkas are made, leave to cool, then tear into small pieces and set aside.

Coarsely grind chillies and garlic, add coriander leaves and grind to thick paste.

Add dry spices, shredded phulkas and mix well.

Heat oil in *kadhai*, add phulka mix, saute for five minutes.

Add water, cover and cook for 10–15 minutes on medium flame.

Remove and serve.

□

SAAG

Raswara Methi-Patata

(Fenugreek Potatoes)

Ingredients

Fenugreek leaves	1½ cup	finely chopped
Potatoes (medium)	4	cut into small pieces
Garlic	5–6 cloves	crushed
Ginger	½ tsp	grated
Tomato (large)	1	chopped
Green chillies	2	
Turmeric powder	1 tsp	
Coriander powder	1 tsp	
Red chilli powder	1 tsp	
Raw mango powder	2 tsp	
Salt	to taste + ¼ cup to clean fenugreek leaves	

To cook

Water	2 ¼ cups
Mustard oil	3–4 tbsp

Method

Add ¼ cup salt to the fenugreek leaves, toss to mix well and set aside.

After half an hour, gently squeeze moisture out and wash at least three to four times.

Pressure-cook for 1 whistles in 2 cups of water. Remove and drain.

Heat oil in flat pan, lightly fry the potatoes, drain from oil and set aside.

In the same pan, saute garlic, ginger, tomatoes and green chillies.

Then add turmeric, coriander and chilli powder and stir well.

Add boiled fenugreek leaves and fried potatoes, stirring well.

Add remaining water, bring to boil, cover and simmer for about five minutes.

Sprinkle mango powder, stir and serve.

Serving tip

Goes well with both roti and rice.

□

Saraya Jo Saag
(Mustard Leaf Saag)

Ingredients

Mustard leaves	1 cup	chopped
Spinach	1 cup	chopped
Fenugreek leaves	1 cup	chopped
Bathua spinach	1 cup	chopped
Spring garlic	½ cup	finely chopped
Ginger	1 tsp	grated
Green chillies	3	finely chopped
Tomatoes (medium)	2	ground into paste
Turmeric powder	1 tsp	
Coriander powder	1 tsp	
Raw mango powder	1 tsp	
Red chilli powder	1 tsp	
Salt	to taste	

To cook

Water	2–3 cups
Mustard oil	6 tbsp

For tadka

Ghee	3 tbsp
Whole red chillies	2

Method

Pressure-cook mustard, spinach, fenugreek and wild spinach leaves in lightly-salted water for four to five whistles. Remove and drain.

When cool, grind coarsely in blender and set aside.

Heat oil in *kadhai*, add spring garlic, ginger, chillies and tomato paste. Bhuno (fry) masala, then add dry spices and stir well.

Add the ground saag and leave to cook for five minutes.

Tadka
Heat ghee in tadka pan, add red chillies.
Drown in saag and cover instantly.

Serving tip
Goes well with jvar and makkai rotis.

□

Palli Jo Saag
(Green Chickpea Leaf Saag)

Ingredients

Chickpea leaves	1½ cup	finely chopped
Tomato (large)	1½	chopped
Ginger	2-inch piece	finely chopped
Garlic	12 cloves	finely chopped
Green chillies	3	finely chopped
Turmeric powder	¾ tsp	
Coriander powder	¾ tsp	
Red chilli powder	¾ tsp	
Raw mango powder	¾ tsp	
Salt	to taste	

To cook

Water	3 cups
Ghee	4 tbsp

For tadka

Ghee	3 tbsp
Whole red chillies	2

Method

Pressure-cook saag in 1½ cup of mildly salted water. Drain, cool and mash.
Heat ghee in a *kadhai*, add ginger, garlic, green chillies and saute lightly.
Mix in tomato and dry spices, and bhuno (fry).
Add saag, ½ cup water, cover and cook for about 10 minutes, then mash it.

Tadka

Heat ghee in tadka pan, add whole red chillies. Drown in saag and cover instantly.

Serving tip

Goes well with jvar or bajra roti.

□

Saraya Jo Saag (Mustard Leaf Saag) • *P-74*

Palli Jo Saag (Green Chickpea Leaf Saag) • *P-76*

Khatti Dal (Tamarind Dal)

• P-80

Teen Dal (Three Dal Blend)

• P-81

Kulfa Saag
(Purslane Leaf Saag)

Ingredients

Purslane leaves	2 cups	finely chopped
Onion (large)	1½	finely chopped
Green chillies	3	
Bengal gram dal	¾ cup	
Tomato (large)	1½	chopped
Turmeric powder	¾ tsp	
Coriander powder	¾ tsp	
Red chilli powder	¾ tsp	
Raw mango powder	¾ tsp	
Salt	to taste	

To cook

Oil	3½ tbsp
Water	1 cup

For tadka

Ghee	3½ tbsp	
Garlic	7–8 cloves	finely chopped
Ginger	2 tsp	grated

Method

Heat oil in pressure cooker pan, add onion and saute lightly.

Add chillies, Bengal gram dal, tomato, purslane leaves and dry spices and mix well.

Add ½ cup water and pressure-cook for three whistles.

Allow to cool, open and lightly mash saag.

Tadka

Heat ghee in tadka pan, add ginger and garlic dry spices.

When nicely brown, drown in saag and cover.

Serving tip

Goes well with khichdi or plain rice. □

LEGUMES & LENTILS

Chana Dal

(Bengal gram dal)

Ingredients

Bengal gram dal	2 cups	
Green chillies	3	finely chopped
Turmeric powder	½ tsp	
Salt	to taste	

To cook

Water	1½ cups

For tadka

Ghee	3 tbsp
Black cumin	1 tsp

To garnish

Onion (medium)	1	finely chopped
Coriander powder	1 tbsp	
Red chilli powder	1 tbsp	
Raw mango powder	2 tbsp	
Fresh coriander	½ cup	finely chopped

Method

Soak dal for three to four hours.

Drain and put dal in pressure cooker.

Add turmeric, salt, green chillies and water and pressure-cook for two whistles.

Pour dal in serving bowl. It should not be too thick.

Tadka
Heat ghee in tadka pan, add cumin and brown.
Pour over dal and cover instantly.

Garnish
Sprinkle with onion, coriander, red chilli, and raw mango powder and garnish with fresh coriander leaves.

Serving tip
Goes well with rotis and green chutney on the side.

□

Khatti Dal
(Tamarind dal)

Ingredients

Yellow lentil dal	1 cup	
Green chillies	2	chopped
Tamarind	3–4 tbsp	pulp
Turmeric powder	½ tsp	
Asafoetida	a p-inch	
Fenugreek seeds	1 tsp	
Salt	to taste	
To cook		
Water	2½ cups	boiling
For tadka		
Ghee	2 tbsp	
Cumin	1 tsp	
Whole red chillies	3	
Karhi leaves	2 sprigs	
Coriander powder	½ tsp	
Chilli powder	½ tsp	

Method

Soak dal for two hours.

Boil water in a heavy-base pan.

Drain dal and put dal in boiling water.

Add green chillies, asafoetida, fenugreek seeds and salt.

Cover and cook on medium flame till dal is soft and well cooked.

Add tamarind pulp and leave it to cook at low pressure for two minutes.

Tadka

Heat ghee in tadka pan. Add cumin, red chillies, Karhi leaves, coriander powder and chilli powder.

Drown in dal and cover immediately.

Serving tip

Goes well with rice. □

Teen Dal
(Three dal blend)

Ingredients

Bengal gram dal	¼ cup	
Green gram dal	¼ cup	
Black gram dal	¼ cup	
Green chillies	3	finely chopped
Turmeric powder	pinch	
Salt	to taste	

To cook

Water	1½ cup

For tadka

Ghee	2–3 tsp	
Garlic	6–7 cloves	finely chopped
Cumin seeds	1 tsp	
Coriander powder	2 tsp	

To garnish

Fresh coriander leaves

Method

Soak dals for about two hours, then wash and remove the skin from approximately ½ the moong and urad dals.

Boil water in a heavy-bottom pan, add dals, green chillies, turmeric and salt.

Bring to a boil, then cover and leave to simmer for half an hour till dals are soft and well cooked.

Tadka

Heat ghee in tadka pan, add garlic, cumin and coriander powder.

Drown in dal and cover instantly.

Garnish and serve goes well jwar roti.

□

Moong Dal
(Yellow lentil)

Ingredients

Yellow lentil	2 cups	
Green chilli	3	finely chopped
Turmeric powder	1 tsp	
Coriander powder	1 tbsp	
Raw mango powder	1 tbsp	
Red chilli	1 tbsp	
Salt	to taste	

To cook

Water	1 cup

For tadka

Ghee	2 tbsp
Cumin seeds	1 tsp

To garnish

Garam masala	1 tsp
Fresh coriander	leaves

Method

Soak the yellow lentils for about two hours, then drain and wash.

Boil water in a heavy-bottomed pan, lower heat and add lentils.

Cover the pan and place a weight on the lid to prevent steam from escaping.

Cook for 5 minutes then add turmeric, salt and green chilli.

Cover and leave till lentils are soft and mushy.

Transfer to serving dish and sprinkle raw mango powder, red chilli, coriander powder and garnish with fresh coriander.

Tadka
Heat ghee in tadka pan.
Add cumin and when it turns golden, drown in dal and cover immediately.
Garnish and serve.

Serving tip
Traditionally served with pooris.

□

MEAT & CHICKEN

Sigri Jo Gosht
(Chule ka Mutton)

Ingredients

Mutton	400 gm	small pieces
Onions (medium)	3	chopped
Garlic	6 cloves	crushed
Green chillies	3	finely chopped
Tomato (large)	1½	chopped
Curd	¾ cup	
Turmeric powder	¾ tsp	
Coriander powder	¾ tsp	
Red chilli powder	¾ tsp	
Black pepper	¾ tsp	
Cinnamon	2-inch stick	
Cloves	5–6	
Black cardamon	1	
Cardamon	5	
Cumin seeds	1 tbsp	
Bay leaves	4	
Salt	to taste	

To cook

Ghee	4½ tbsp

To garnish

Garam masala	1 tbsp

Method

Put the mutton in a heavy-bottom vessel, pour in the ghee and add all the ingredients.

Mix well, cover and set aside for one hour.

Light the coal in the earthen oven and place the vessel on it.

Cover with a heavy lid and place a weight on the lid to prevent steam from escaping.

Leave for three to four hours until cooked.

Sprinkle with garam masala and serve.

Serving tip

Goes well with tandoori roti.

□

Bhugal Gosht
(Masala Mutton)

Ingredients

Mutton	400 gm	nicely chopped
Onion (small)	3	finely chopped
Green chillies	3	finely chopped
Ginger	2-inch piece	
Garlic	9 cloves	
Turmeric powder	¾ tsp	
Coriander powder	¾ tsp	
Red chilli powder	¾ tsp	
Black pepper	¾ tsp	
Cumin corns	1½ tsp	
Cinnamon	2-inch stick	
Cloves	6–7	
Bay leaves	3	

To cook

Ghee	4½ tbsp

To garnish

Garam masala	1 tbsp

Method

Heat ghee in pressure cooker pan on medium heat. Add mutton, chillies, garlic and ginger, stirring well.

Pressure-cook for 1 whistle. Allow to cool, then open.

Heat ghee in *kadhai*, add all the spices and cooked mutton.

Stir and cook till mutton is dry and coated with spices.

Sprinkle with garam masala and serve.

Serving tip

Can also be served on its own as a snack.

□

Pallo Macchi
(Steamed Hilsa)

Ingredients

Hilsa fish	1	
For marinate		
Tamarind pulp	6 tsp	
Turmeric powder	1 tsp	
Red chilli powder	½ tsp	
Salt	to taste	
To cook		
Onion (large)	4	finely chopped
Ginger	1 tsp	paste
Garlic	1 tbsp	paste
Green chillies	6	finely chopped
Coriander powder	1 tbsp	
Red chilli powder	1 tsp	
For tadka		
Ghee	8 tsp	
To garnish		
Garam masala	1 tsp	
Fresh coriander leaves		finely chopped

Method

Take whole fish, clean it and slit vertically from head to tail, leaving the backbone untouched. Also lightly slash the top. Wash and dry thoroughly.

Mix all the ingredients for marinade and rub on the fish both inside and outside. Leave to marinate for about one hour.

Mix onions and dry spies.

Take a clean muslin cloth, large enough to wrap the fish in.

Spread the onion mix on the centre of the cloth and place the marinated fish on it.

Wrap the cloth around the fish and tie it.

Half-fill a *kadhai* with water.

Place some wooden logs in the *kadhai* to form a stand that will keep the fish above the water (you could place a sieve or steamer base upside down).

Place the muslin-wrapped fish on the logs.

Cover the *kadhai* tightly and place a weight to top to keep the steam in.

Leave to cook for 40–50 min. until the aroma signals that the fish is cooked.

Transfer the fish into a serving dish and gently slide the muslin out from *kadhai.*

Heat the ghee to smokey hot in a tempering pan and pour over the fish.

Garnish with garam masala and fresh coriander.

My father-in-law had watched hilsa being cooked like this in Sind in his youth and would replicate the flavours for the family on very special occasions by cooking it for us exactly as he had seen.

□

Macchi Sayel Masale Mein
(Fish in Green Masala)

Ingredients

Fish (boneless)	750 gm	
Green masala	8–9 tbsp	
Green chillies	3	finely chopped
Turmeric powder	1½ tsp	
Coriander powder	1½ tsp	
Red chilli powder	1½ tsp	
Raw mango powder	1½ tsp	
Salt	to taste	

To cook

Mustard oil	4–5 tbsp
Water	3 cups

Method

Apply salt on fish for half an hour then wash it.

Heat oil in a deep pan. Add green masala, chillies and spices and stir well.

Add fish and water.

Cover and cook for 10–15 minutes.

Serving tip

Goes well with rice or roti.

□

Narel Mein Murgo
(Coconut Chicken)

Ingredients

Chicken	750 gm	
Coconut powder	3 tbsp	
Garlic	15–16 cloves	crushed
Green chillies	5	finely chopped
Turmeric powder	1½ tbsp	
Coriander powder	1½ tbsp	
Salt	to taste	

To cook

Mustard oil	3 tbsp

To garnish

Garam masala	¾ tsp

Method

Place the chicken in a bowl, add coconut powder, garlic, chillies, turmeric, salt and mix well.

Cover and set aside to marinade for one hour.

Heat oil in a *kadhai* and add the marinaded chicken.

Cover and leave to cook on low heat until cooked (about 45 minutes).

Sprinkle with garam masala and serve.

Serving tip

Rice and coconut chicken make a great combination.

It can be served as snack.

☐

Sigri Jo Gosht (Chule Ka Mutton) • P-84

Bhugal Gosht (Masala Mutton) • P-86

Macchi Sayel Masale Mein (Fish in Green Masala) • P-89

Basarwari Koki (Onion Koki) • P-91

ROTIS

Basarwari Koki

(Onion Koki)

Ingredients		
Wheat flour	2 cup	
Onion (small)	½	finely chopped
Green chillies	2–3	finely chopped
Fresh coriander	1 cup	finely chopped
Pomegranate seeds	¾ tsp	coarsely ground
Salt	to taste	
Ghee	7–8 tbsp	
Water	3–4 tbsp	
To cook		
Ghee	6 tbsp	to shallow fry

Method

Mix all ingredients and knead into a hard dough. Set aside for 10 minutes.

Divide dough into 6 equal parts, then roll and shape each into a small ball with your hands.

Take a rolling pin and flatten each ball into a thick roti, about 3-inches in diameter.

Place on heated tava and cook lightly on both sides on a medium flame.

Remove from tava and immediately roll again to make thin roti about 5 inches in diameter.

Brush with ghee and put back on tava, ghee-face down.

Brush top surface with ghee and flip.

Cook for one minute or until both sides are lightly golden and koki is crisp.

Serving tip

Goes well with curd and pickle.

□

Karemirchwari Koki
(Black pepper Koki)

Ingredients

Wheat flour	2 cup	
Black pepper	2 tsp	coarsely ground
Black cumin	1½ tsp	
Ghee	6–7 tsp	
Salt	to taste	
Water	3–4 tbsp	

To cook

Ghee	6 tbsp	to shallow fry

Method

Mix all ingredients and knead into a hard dough. Set aside for 10 minutes.

Divide dough into 6 equal parts, then roll and shape each into a small ball with your hands.

Take a rolling pin and flatten each ball into a circle, about 3 inches in diameter.

Place on heated tava and cook lightly on both sides on a medium flame.

Remove from tava and roll again to make thinner roti about 5 inches in diameter.

Brush with ghee and put back on tava ghee face down.

Brush top surface with ghee and flip.

Cook for one minute or until both sides are lightly golden.

Serving tip

Goes well with curd and pickle.

□

Karemirchwari Koki (Black Pepper Koki) • P-92

Besanji Koki (Gram Flour Koki) • P-93

Dal Pakwan

• *P-94*

Moong Dal Parantha (Yellow Lentil Stuffed Flatbread)

• *P-95*

Besanji Koki
(Gram flour Koki)

Ingredients

Gram flour	2 cup	
Green chillies	4–5	finely chopped
Onion	1	finely chopped
Coriander powder	¾ tsp	
Red chilli powder	¾ tsp	
Pomegranate powder	¾ tsp	
Coriander seeds	¾ tsp	
Fresh coriander leaves	¾ tsp	
Zeera	¾ tsp	
Ghee	6–8 tsp	
Water	3–4 tbsp	
Salt	to taste	

To cook

Ghee	6 tbsp	to shallow fry

Method

Mix all ingredients and knead into a hard dough. Set aside for 10 minutes.

Divide dough into 6 equal parts, then roll and shape each into a small ball with your hands.

Take a rolling pin and flatten each ball into a thick roti, about 3 inches in diameter.

Remove from tava and roll again to make thinner roti about 5 inches in diameter.

Brush with ghee and put back on tava ghee face down.

Brush top surface with ghee and flip.

Cook for one minute or until both sides are lightly golden.

Serving tip

Goes well with curd and pickle.

□

Pakwan

(Fried flatbread)

Ingredients

All-purpose flour	1 cup
Carom seeds	1 tsp
Ghee	1 tbsp
Salt	to taste
Water	3–4 tbsp

To cook

Oil	to deep fry

Method

Mix flour, carom seeds and salt well, then rub in the oil.

Add water and knead well into a hard dough.

Break off small portions of the dough and roll into small balls, flatten and then roll out into very thin circles (about 6 inches in diameter).

Take a fork and press the tines into the dough.

Roll out all the balls.

Heat oil in a *kadhai*, turn flame to medium and deep fry each separately till golden.

Serving tip

The traditional combination is pakwan and charanji dal green chutney and onion salad.

□

Moong Dal Parantha
(Yellow lentil stuffed flatbread)

Ingredients

Yellow lentil dal	½ cup	
Whole wheat flour	1½ cup	
Green chillies	2	finely chopped
Cumin	½ spoon	
Red chilli powder	½ spoon	
Raw mango powder	1 tsp	
Salt	to taste	
Water for dough	½ –¾ cup	

To cook

Ghee	½ cup	to shallow fry
Water to boil dal	1½ cup	

Method

Boil the dal in a pot, not in a pressure cooker, with a p-inch of salt until soft but not mushy. Then drain out the excess water and set aside to cool.

Knead a soft dough and set aside.

When the dal is cool enough to handle mix in green and red chillies, cumin, raw mango powder and salt, then divide into six portions.

Set the tava to heat.

Divide dough into six portions then roll and shape each into a small ball with your hands.

Take a rolling pin and roll one portion out into a slightly thick circle, about 4 inches in diameter.

Lightly spread a little ghee on it, then spread one portion of dal.

Sprinkle dry atta over dal then gently fold to form a ball.

Roll out again with the rolling pin to about 5-inch diameter.

Place on the tava and turn down the heat to a medium flame.

Cook one side for about a minute, then flip.
Spread the top with ghee, flip again, and spread ghee on this side as well.
Shallow fry until golden and crisp, then take off tava.
Repeat till all portions are done.

Serving tip
Paranthas, curd and pickle make for a classic combination.

□

Sayel Masalewari Macchi Biryani (Green Fish Biryani)

• P-97

Hyderabadi Murg Biryani (Hyderabadi Chicken Biryani) • P-98

Sindhi Gosht Biryani (Sindhi Mutton Biryani) • P-100

BIRYANIS

Sayel Masalewari Macchi Biryani

(Green Fish Biryani)

Ingredients

Rice	1 cup	Basmati is best
Fish (rohu)	7–8 pieces	
Turmeric powder	¼ tsp	
Green masala	1 cup	
Salt	to taste	
Raw mango powder	½ tsp	
To cook		
Water	3 cups	
To garnish		
Spring onion	¼ cup	finely chopped
For tadka		
Ghee	1/3 cup	

Method

Mix turmeric and raw mango powder in green masala, thoroughly coat fish and leave to marinade for half an hour.

Parboil rice with salt in 3 cups of water.

Drain rice, leaving about three to four tablespoons of water and add the fish.

Cover and cook on slow flame till fish is done.

Transfer to serving dish and garnish with spring onion.

Heat ghee in tadka pan, pour over biryani and serve.

□

Hyderabadi Murg Biryani
(Hyderabadi Chicken Biryani)

Ingredients

Rice	1 cup	Basmati is best
Chicken with bones	750 gms	cut in small pieces
Ginger	1-inch piece	finely chopped
Garlic	5–6 cloves	finely chopped
Cinnamon	1½ -inch stick	
Cloves	2–3	
Black peppercorn	8–9	
Bay leaves	2–3	
Cumin seeds	1 tsp	
Onion (medium)	4	thinly sliced
Green chillies	2–3	finely chopped
Coriander powder	1 tbs	
Red chilli powder	1 tbs	
Salt	to taste	
Curd	½ cup	whipped smooth
Saffron	7–8 strands	soaked in milk
Milk	¼ cup	
Kevra	8–9 drops	
Garam masala	1 tbs	

To cook

Ghee	½ cup
Water (to parboil rice)	3 cups
(for chicken)	¼ cup

Method

Soak rice for half an hour, then parboil with salt in three cups of water, drain and set aside.

Heat ghee in a pan.

Fry onion till golden-brown, take-out half and set aside.

To the remaining onions, add chicken, ginger, garlic, green chillies, all the dry masalas and stir well.

Add water and cook on medium flame till chicken is tender.

Take a heavy, flat-bottom pan and layer the bottom with rice.

Cover with pieces of chicken, pour whipped curd over them and sprinkle half the fried onions on top.

Add a layer of rice, sprinkle saffron milk, then spread pieces of chicken.

Top with a final layer of rice, sprinkle kevra, garam masala and top with remaining fried onions.

Cover pan and cook on a low flame for two minutes.

Serving tip

A raita of whipped curd and boondi is the perfect accompaniment.

□

Sindhi Gosht Biryani

(Sindhi Mutton Biryani)

Ingredients

Rice	1½ cup	Basmati is best
Mutton	400 gm	cut in small pieces
Onions (medium)	4½	sliced
Green chillies	3	chopped
Tomatoes (medium)	3	chopped
Garlic	8–9 cloves	finely chopped
Ginger	1-inch piece	finely chopped
Cinnamon	1½ -inch stick	
Cloves	5–6	
Bay leaves	2	
Black peppercorn	8–10	
Cumin seeds	1½ tsp	
Coriander powder	1½ tbs	
Red chilli powder	1½ tbs	
Salt	to taste	

To cook

Water	3 cups	boiling
Ghee	¾ cup	

To garnish

Mint leaves	7–8 leaves
Garam masala	¾ tsp

Method

Soak rice for about half an hour.

Heat ½ cup ghee in a heavy-bottomed pan, saute onions, then add chilli, ginger, garlic, tomatoes and whole masalas and saute.

Add mutton and salt.

Cover and cook on medium flame till mutton is tender.

Wash and drain rice, and add to mutton.

Add red chilli and coriander powder, mix well and then add boiling water.

Cover and leave to cook on medium flame.

Transfer to serving dish and garnish with garam masala and mint leaves and fried onions.

Heat remaining ghee in tadka pan and pour over biryani.

Serving tip

Goes well with onion or mixed vegetable raita.

□

CONDIMENTS—CHUTNEY, ACHAR, MURBA

Achari Masala Bharyal Sava Mirch
(Stuffed Green Chillies)

Ingredients

Long green chillies	6
Mango powder	1 tsp
Mango pickle masala	3 tsp

To cook

Mustard oil	1 tbsp

Method

Slit the chillies along one length and carefully remove the seeds.

Wash, pat dry then gently rub with salt both inside and out and set aside for 10 minutes.

Heat oven to 180°C.

Thoroughly mix mango powder and mango pickle masala and stuff chillies.

Brush oven tray with oil and place chillies on it.

Bake till golden in colour and serve.

Alternatively, grill or cook on non-stick tava.

□

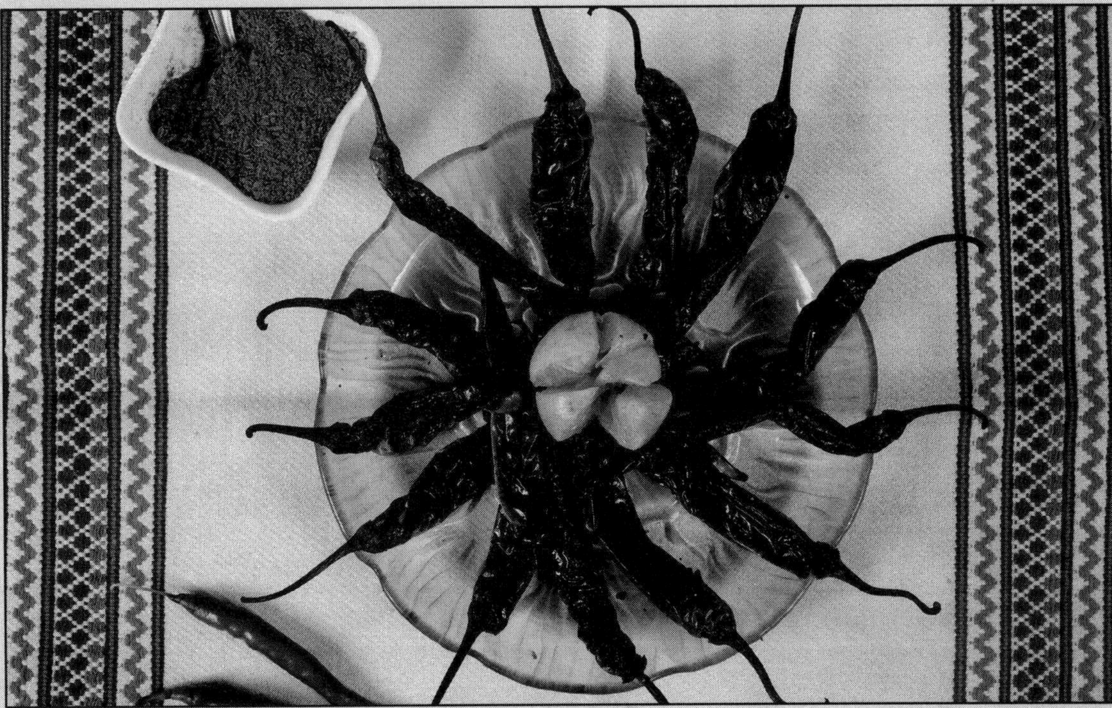

Achari Masala Bharyal Sava Mirch (Stuffed Green Chillies) • P-102

Gidamariji Chutney (Sweet Tamarind Chutney) • P-104

Sai Chutney (Green Chutney) • P-105

Ambri Jo Achar (Mango Pickle) • P-107

Ambri Basarji Chutney
(Raw mango & Onion Chutney)

Ingredients

Raw mango (small)	1	chopped
Onion (medium)	2	chopped
Mint	2–3 sprigs	
Red chilli powder	1tsp	
Green chilli	1	chopped
Salt	to taste	

Method

Place all ingredients in a grinder and make a coarse paste.

□

Gidamariji Chutney
(Sweet Tamarind Chutney)

Ingredients

Tamarind pulp	2 cups
Jaggery	3 cups
Ginger powder	½ tsp
Chilli powder	½ tsp
Cumin powder	½ tsp
Garam masala	½ tsp
Salt	to taste

Method

Melt jaggery in tamarind pulp, adding a little water if needed.
Then add spices and salt and leave to simmer until the chutney thickens.

Options to add

Raisins	10–15
Watermelon seeds	1 tbs

Serving tip

The sweet-sour combination is a great teaser of taste buds—so dip chips in it or pour it over curd.

□

Sai Chutney
(Green Chutney)

Ingredients

Coriander	1½ cup
Mint	½ cup
Green chillies	7–8
Roasted channa dal	1 tbsp
Boondi	3–4 tsp
Water	2–3 tbs
Ginger	1-inch piece grated
Jeera	1 tsp
Lemon juice	2–3 tbsp
Rock salt	1 tsp

Method

Place all ingredients in a grinder and make a smooth paste.

Serving tip

This is a highly versatile chutney. In addition to pepping up pakoras, samosas and cutlets, it also makes an excellent dip and an interesting spread for sandwich.

□

Leemeji Chutney
(Lemon Chutney)

Ingredients

Lemons	8
Salt	3 tsp
Black cardamom powder	1
Cloves	2–3
Red chili powder	¼ tsp
Sugar	1½ cup

Method

Thoroughly wash the lemons and extract the juice.
Remove the pulp and discard it.
Turn the skin inside out and cut into thin flakes.
Put the flakes in the juice and add salt.
Cover tightly and place in the sun for four-to five days.
Add sugar and remaining ingredients. Pour this into an airtight container.
Leave to soak for another 15–16 days, shaking regularly.

□

Ambri Jo Achar
(Mango Pickle)

Ingredients

Raw mango	2½ kg
Asafoetida	a pinch
Mustard seeds	½ cup
Fenugreek seeds	¼ cup
Fennel seeds	½ cup
Onion seeds	½ cup
Carom seeds	2 tbsp
Salt	¾ cup
Mustard oil	2 cups

Method

Wash the mangoes thoroughly and gently rub dry with a soft cloth.
Cut into small, 1 inch long pieces and remove the seed.
Grind all the spices coarsely.
Heat all the oil in a *kadhai* (wok) till it is smoking hot.
Remove from fire and allow the wok to cool.
Take about 3–4 tbsp of oil and mix in the spices.
Coat the mango pieces with these spices.
Put the mango pieces in a ceramic or glass jar.
Pour in the remaining mustard oil.
Close tightly and shake well.
Place in direct sunlight for a week, shaking well twice a day.

□

Amb Jo Murabo
(Mango Preserve)

Ingredients

Mango (preferably Totapuri)	1 kg
Lime juice	2 tbsp
Water	6 cups
Alum	1½ tsp
Sugar	5 cups
Black cardamom (crushed)	2
Yellow food colour	2–3 drops
Almonds (chopped)	10–12
Citric acid powder	¼ tsp
Sal ammoniac	¼ tsp

Method

Wash and skin the mangoes, then cut into thick, wide slices.

Use a fork and gently prick holes in the slices and pour lime juice over them.

Place in a shallow bowl, cover with water and leave to soak overnight.

Wash thoroughly to remove all lime juice.

Soak again for 12 hours; then strain the liquid.

Boil in 2 cups of water with alum and sal ammoniac till tender.

Drain, cool and wash well to remove any smell.

Boil sugar in 4 cups of water till it becomes sticky.

Add mango slices and cardamom and leave for 12 hours.

Add yellow food colour and almonds. Cook with citric acid for 5 minutes.

Make sure the syrup covers the mango.

□

Leeme Jo Achar Masale Waro
(Lemon Pickle With Spice)

Ingredients

Lemons	8
Salt	1¼ cup
Sugar	¾ cup
Garam masala	1 tsp
Red chili powder	1 tbsp
Cardamom powder	1 tsp

Method

Wash lemons properly and cut into four pieces.
Put these pieces into a ceramic or glass jar.
Add salt, cover tightly and shake well.
Leave in direct sunlight for four days, shaking occasionally.
Then mix all the other ingredients and pour into a jar.
Close tightly and shake.
Leave to stand for seven to eight days before serving.

□

Leeme Jo Achar
(Lemon and Salt Pickle)

Ingredients

Lemons	8
Salt	¾ cup

Method

Wash lemons well. Make deep cuts in each with a knife.
Place lemons in a ceramic or glass jar and add the salt.
Cover tightly and shake well.
Leave in direct sunlight for 15–20 days before serving.

This pickle is very good for digestion and highly restorative in case of loose motions.

□

Pani Waro Basar Jo Achar
(Onions Pickled in Water)

Ingredients

Baby onions	30–35 gm
Mustard seeds powder	2 tbsp
Turmeric powder	1 tbsp
Red chili powder	1 tbsp
Salt	1 cup
Water	5 cups

Method

Peel the onions. Make four deep cuts in each onion.
Wash and transfer into a glass jar.
Add salt, spices and mix well.
Pour in enough water to cover the onions.
Close tightly and leave in direct sunlight for two days and serve.
Keep in the refrigerator and finish within two to three days.

☐

Pani Wariyoon Gajar Achar
(Pickled Carrots in Water)

Ingredients

Carrots (cut into long thin slices)	2
Mustard powder	2 tbsp

Method

Blanch carrot slices and immediately transfer to cold water.
Drain and put in a ceramic or glass jar.
Add all other ingredients except water and shake thoroughly.
Add water.
Close lid and place in direct sunlight for two days before serving.

☐

Amb Jo Murabo (Mango Preserve) • P-108

Leeme Jo Achar Masale Waro (Lemon Pickle with Spice) • P-109

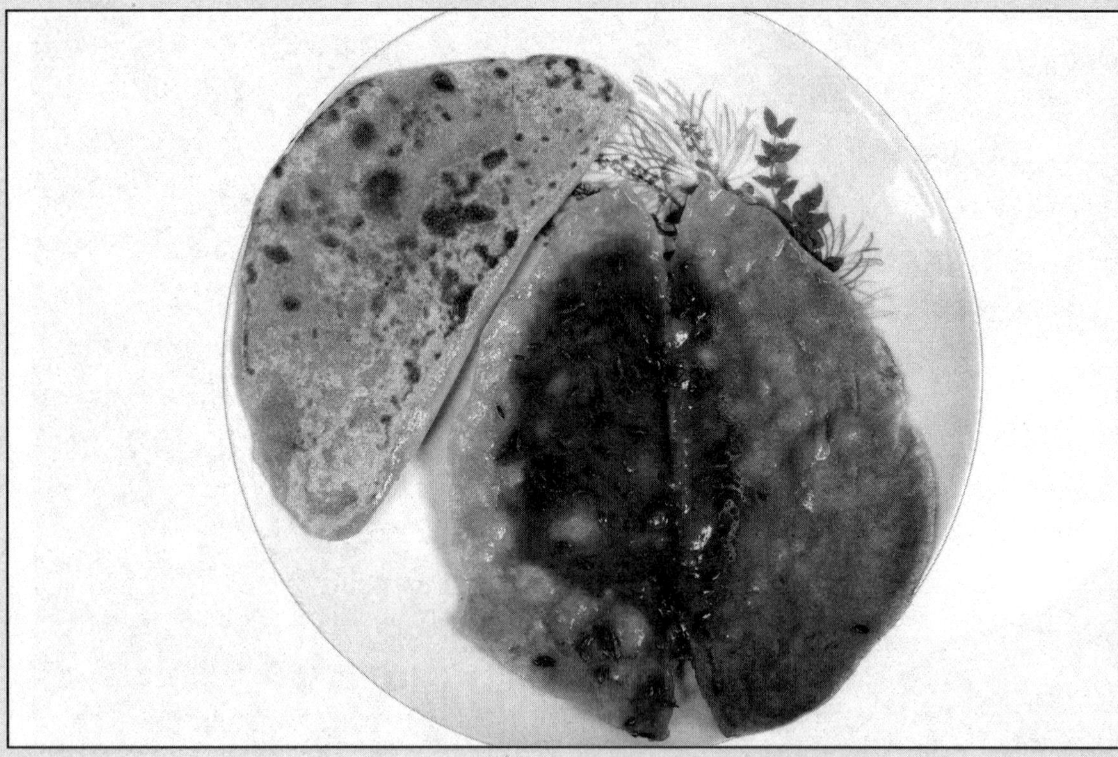

Gudji Roti (Stuffed Jaggery Flatbread) • P-114

Malpuro (Fried Sweet Pancake) • P-115

Gajrun Jo Achar
(Carrot Pickle)

Ingredients

Carrots (medium)	6
Mustard seeds	5 tsp
Fennel seeds	4 tsp
Cumin seeds	2 tsp
Black pepper powder	½ tsp
Black salt	½ tsp
Red chili powder	3 tsp
Turmeric powder	2 tsp
Onion seeds	1 tsp
Mustard oil	3 ½ cups
Salt	8 tsp

Method

Peel the carrots and carefully slit them lengthwise to create a pouch.

Take 2 tsp of salt and rub on carrots, both inside and out.

Leave for 15 minutes. Wash them well and dry with a soft cloth.

Mix all ingredients, except the oil and fill inside the carrots.

Put the carrots in a ceramic or glass jar.

Pour the oil cover the carrots.

Place in direct sunlight for about ten days, gently shaking the jar occasionally.

□

DESSERTS

Gudji Roti
(Stuffed Jaggery Flatbread)

Ingredients

Whole wheat flour	1 cup	
Water	¼ cup	
Jaggery	3 tbs	grated
Fennel	1½ tsp	
Carom seeds	¾ tsp	
Salt	a pinch	

To cook

Ghee	6 tbsp

Method

Knead into a soft dough adding water as needed.

Divide dough into 4 and roll each portion into a ball between the palms.

Take each ball and use a rolling pin to flatten it to an 8–9-inch circle.

Sprinkle half the circle with jaggery, fennel and carom seeds, then spread ¼ tsp ghee.

Fold and cover with other half.

Place on heated tava, brush with ghee and cook both sides on low heat till golden.

Open fold, pour a little ghee inside and serve.

□

Malpuro
(Fried Sweet Pancake)

Ingredients

Whole wheat flour	1 cup	
Sugar	4 tbs	powdered
Water	½ cup	hot
Almonds	6	powdered
Cardamom	½ tsp	crushed
Fennel	½ tsp	

To cook

Ghee	to deep fry

Method

Melt sugar in hot water.

Mix almonds, cardamom and fennel in the flour.

Add sugar water and beat into a batter of dropping consistency.

Heat ghee in a *kadhai*.

Pour a tablespoon of batter in the centre of the *kadhai* and deep fry on medium flame, turning sides till malpuro is golden brown. Strain and take out.

Pour another tablespoon of batter and fry malpuro, one by one until done.

Serve hot.

□

Meethyoo Sayoon
(Sweet Vermicelli)

Ingredients

Roasted vermicelli (fine)	1½ cup	
Water	1½ cup	
Sugar	½ cup	
Cardamom	¾ tsp	crushed
Almonds	12–15	chopped

To cook

Ghee	2 tbs

Method

Heat ghee in a *kadhai* on medium heat. Add vermicelli and stir till golden.
Pour water and boil.
When vermicelli starts to dry, add sugar, cardamom and almonds.
Cover and leave to cook on low heat for five minutes.
Serve hot.

□

Meethyoo Sayoon (Sweet Vermicelli) • P-116

Meetho Bhatt (Sweet Porridge) • P-117

Khumb (Vermicelli Pudding) • P-118

Lolo (Sweet Flatbread) • P-119

Meetho Bhatt
(Sweet Porridge)

Ingredients

Wheat porridge	1½ cup	
Sugar	½ cup	
Cardamom powder	1/3 tsp	crushed
Almonds	12	chopped

To cook

Ghee	5 tbs	
Water	4½ cups	boiling

Method

Heat ghee in a pressure cooker pan on medium heat, Add porridge and roast till golden.

Add boiling water and pressure-cook for 2 whistles, then lower flame and cook for five minutes more.

Cool, open and add sugar, cardamom, and almonds and mix well.

Leave on low flame for 2 minutes, then pour into serving bowl.

Serve hot.

☐

Khumb
(Vermicelli Pudding)

Ingredients

Milk	4 cups	full cream is always better
Sugar	1 cup	
Sevian	1/3 cup	preferably the thick, homemade variety
Salt	a tiny pinch	
Cardamon	¼ tsp	powdered
Nuts	¼ cup	almonds, walnuts, pistachio, coarsely crushed
Saffron	15–20 threads	soaked in about 1 tbsp milk

Method

Set the milk to boil in a heavy-bottomed pot.
Once it boils turn down the flame and leave to simmer.
After about 20 minutes add sevian.
Stir occasionally till sevian is cooked.
Add sugar, salt, cardamon, nuts and saffron and take off flame.
Serve hot or cold.

□

Lolo
(Sweet Flatbread)

Ingredients

Whole wheat flour	3 cups	
Jaggery	1 cup	crushed
Water	¼ cup	lukewarm
Cardamon	1 tsp	ground
Ghee	1 cup	

To cook

Ghee	6 tsp

Method

Melt the jaggery in the hot water.

Mix the cardamon in the atta, then gently rub the in ghee until the atta forms granules.

Gradually add the melted jaggery and knead into a tight dough.

Set aside for 10 minutes to breathe till it becomes smooth.

Put a tava to heat on medium flame.

Divide dough into 6 and roll each portion into a ball.

Use a rolling pin to roll out 6 thick rotis about 6 inches in diameter.

Use the tines of a fork to make shallow indentations on the surface of each.

Put a roti on the hot tava and cook on a low flame.

Keeping moving the roti about, brushing it with ghee and turning it on the tava so that it cooks evenly and becomes crisp.

Plate the lolo, drop a little ghee on top and serve.

Serving tip

Delicious with curd.

□

Gudji Kutti

(Sweet Whole wheat Flatbread)

Ingredients

Whole wheat flour	1½ cup	
Jaggery	¾ cup	
Ghee	¾ cup	
Water	1 cup	
Almonds	8–10	blanched and chopped
Cardamon powder	1 tsp	

Method

Knead atta into a soft dough with ½ cup water and set aside to breathe for 10 minutes.

Heat tava, divide the dough into seven to eight portions and make very soft rotis.

Leave to cool then crumble the rotis.

Heat ghee in a *kadhai* on medium flame.

Add jaggery and ½ cup water and keep stirring till jaggery dissolves.

Add the crumbled rotis, almonds and cardamon and mix well.

Serve hot.

Serving tip

Very enjoyable with Sindhi papad.

□

Gudji Kutti (Sweet Whole Wheat Flatbread) • *P-120*

Lahori Gajjar (Sweet Potato in Syrup) • *P-121*

Khuskhus Jo Siro (Poppyseed Halwa) • *P-122*

Mohan Thal (Chickpea-Flour Squares) • *P-123*

Lahori Gajjar
(Sweet potato in Syrup)

Ingredients

Sweet potato (medium)	5	
Jaggery	1/3 cup	
Cardamom	1 tsp	crushed
Almonds	12	blanched

To cook

Water	1 cup

Method

Boil sweet potatoes. Peel, then slice into circular pieces and set aside.
Boil water in a *kadhai* and add jaggery to make a thin syrup.
Add sweet potatoes, cardamom, almonds, and simmer for two minutes.
Serve hot.

Khuskhus Jo Siro
(Poppyseed Halwa)

Ingredients

Poppy seeds	1 cup
Milk	2 cups
Sugar	½ cup
Salt	a pinch
Cardamon	4–5

To cook

Ghee (clarified butter)	3 tbsp

To garnish

Almonds and pistachio flakes

Method

Soak poppy seeds overnight.
Wash them properly twice or thrice in clean water.
Grind them into a fine paste.
Heat ghee in a *kadhai* on medium heat.
Add poppy seed paste and dry fry till the edges curl outside.
Add milk and keep stirring till it is absorbed.
Add sugar and salt and stir for another two to three minutes.
Transfer to a serving dish, garnish and serve.

□

Mohan Thal
(Chickpea-Flour Squares)

Ingredients

Chickpea flour	2 cups	
Ghee	1 cup	
Milk	¾ cup	
Water	1 cup	
Sugar	1 cup	
Almonds and pistachio	15–20	chopped fine

Method

Put chickpea flour in a bowl and rub in 3 tbsp ghee.
Add 3 tbsp of milk and rub in thoroughly with fingers.
Transfer into a dry grinder and make into a coarse powder.
Heat water in a pan and add sugar and boil to make a syrup.
Place a *kadhai* on low heat.
Add remaining ghee and chickpea flour powder.
Roast the mixture until it emits an aroma, stirring continuously.
Cook till golden brown.
Add milk and keep stirring till it is absorbed.
Add the syrup and nuts and stir in well.
Pour onto a tray and leave to cool and set.
Cut into squares and serve.

□

Glossary

English	Sindhi	Hindi
All-purpose flour	Maido	Maida
Corn flour	Makkai atto	Makkai atta
Gram/chickpea flour	Besan	Besan
Pearl millet	Bajhri atto	Bajra atta
Sorghum	Juar atto	Jvar atta
Whole wheat flour	Atto	Atta
Spices		
Sal ammonic	नौशादर	Nausadar
Asafoetida	Heeng	Heeng
Bay leaf	Kamaal patto	Tez patta
Black cardamom	Vada phota	Bari ilaichi
Black cumin	Suraih jiri	Kala zeera
Cardamom	Nandha phota	Choti ilaichi
Carom	Jaanr	Ajwain
Clove	Laung	Laung
Coriander (seeds/powder)	Dharan	Dhania
Cumin (seeds/powder)	Jeero	Jeera
Black Salt	Karo Loon	Kala Namak
Fennel	Saunf	Saunf
Fenugreek	Hurbho	Methi
Mace	Javitri	Javitri

Mustard seed	Aur	Rai
Nutmeg	Jaiphal	Jaiphal
Citric-acid powder	Tatri	Tatri Nimbu
Pomegranate powder	Daru khatta pithal	Anardana pissa
Raw mango powder	Ambchur	Amchur
Red pepper	Gadha mirch	Lal mirch
Saffron	Kesar	Kesar
Salt	Loonr	Namak
Tamarind	Gidamiri	Imli
Turmeric	Haid	Haldi
Alum	Phitki	Phitkari
Herbs		
Onion seeds	Basar Jo Bhij	Kalonji
Poppy seeds	Khus Khus	Khus Khus
Coriander leaves	Sava dhana (kotmir)	Hara dhaniya
Karhi leaves	Meethi neem	Kari patta
Garlic	Thoom	Lassan
Ginger	Adrak	Adrak
Green chilli	Sava mirch	Hari mirch
Mint leaves	Pudino	Pudina
Spring garlic	Sai thoom	Hara lassan
Spring onion	Sava basar	Hara pyaz
Vegetables		
Brinjal/aubergine/eggplant	Vangan	Baigan
Capsicum	Simla mirch	Simla mirch
Chickpea leaves	Palli	Chana saag
Cluster beans	Gwar	Guar
Dried mushrooms	Dhingri	Dhingri
Fenugreek leaves	Methi	Methi

Indian squash/apple gourd	Meha	Tinda
Jackfruit	Kathal	Kathal
Lotus stem	Bheeh	Kamalkakdi
Mustard leaves	Sarya	Sarson ka saag
Okra/ladyfinger	Bheendiyun	Bhindi
Onion	Basar	Piyaz
Potato	Patata	Aloo
Purslane leaves	Loonrak	Kulfa
Ridge gourd	Tooriyun	Tori
Spinach	Palak	Palak
Sweet potato	Lahori gajjar	Shakkarkandi
Wild spinach/Lamb's quarter	Bathua	Bathua
Pulses		
Black gram skinned split	Mahen ji dal	Urad dal
Bengal gram spilt and skinned Charan ji dal	Channa dal	Channa dal
Green gram	Moong chhilke wari dal	Moong chhilka dal
Yellow lentils	Moong dhotal dal	Moong dhuli
Black gram	Kara channa	Kala channa
Chickpeas/white gram	Achha channa	Chhole
Other		
Buns plain, unsweetened	Dhabal	Pao
Cottage cheese	Paneer	Paneer
Curd/yoghurt	Dhudh	Dahi
Jaggery	Gud	Gur
Vermicelli	Sayoon	Sevian
Whole wheat porridge	Bhatt	Daliya

□□□